Praise for Fiona Harrold

'With Fiona on your side, you can achieve anything. Whether it's through her books, articles or in person, she has the gift of making everyone feel 100 per cent better about themselves. Truly inspirational!'
Karen Swayne, *Prima* magazine

'Fiona's talent is to ask exactly the right questions to let you see the way forward. The answers to your problems become obvious and, one by one, they are overcome until you have a clear view of what you want from life, and a clear route to achieving it.'
Kay Cox, *Daily Record*

'I phoned Fiona looking for some "wind beneath my wings" and ended up with a Force Ten storm. Within a fortnight of confiding in her my childhood ambition to write novels I'd completed the first chapter of *Re-inventing Tara*. Today that very first manuscript is a Time Warner paperback and I'm living my dream of being a full-time novelist. I'll always be grateful to Fiona for helping me make it happen so quickly.'
Lennox Morrison, novelist

'Fiona Harrold promotes self-discovery with such passion and conviction that "tomorrow" drops from your vocabulary. She'll challenge you with such effectiveness that however big the fairytale, whatever the dream, the only option is to live it.'
Fiona Campbell, designer

'Coaching is essential in any game and vital in the game of life. Fiona is a visionary whose ability as a lifecoach puts her at the top of the premier league. Fiona must be congratulated on getting life coaching onto the map – it is here to stay and needs to be integrated into most health care programmes.'
Mr Michael Dooley, MMS FRCOG, Consultant Gynaecologist

'Fiona gets you to cut through the crap and focus on the real issues. Once you can do that life becomes a lot simpler! The rest is up to you . . .'
Philip Joisce, MD, Goode International

'Working with Fiona radically changed the way I looked at my life. I used to feel that there was always a reason why I couldn't do something. Now, I feel there isn't anything I couldn't do if I wanted to. I also feel that my life fits me and I'm ready to enjoy the rest of my life.'
Angus McLean, property developer

'Inspirational. An hour and half with Fiona changed my perspective on life and my position in it beyond recognition! Above all, her belief in me and my potential gave me the lift I needed to stand up and be counted. Without a doubt, a life changing experience.'
Nina Lockwood, MD, Stroll Limited

'Above all, I found that Fiona helped me quickly reach clarity on complex life decisions. She had an uncanny talent for cutting straight to the essential elements of my life and my character, and causing me to arrive at home truths about them – and to act on those truths. Three months after working

with her I had bought a new home and moved into a position as CEO of a sizeable European company.'
David Jones, chief executive officer

'I wanted a career change, within two weeks I was clear about the way forward! Working with Fiona has been transforming, she has brought great clarity to my complex "stuff", which has enabled me to move forward from the crossroads and embark on a massive change in lifestyle that really excites me. Fiona is liberating and empowering.'
Eleanor McNellan, MD, Eleanor McNellan Designs

'Working with Fiona is setting me free to fulfil my potential and gain far greater enjoyment in all aspects of my life. Fiona's enthusiasm, relentless positivity and ability to listen, understand and suggest action points that "hit the spot" have served to substantially increase my self-belief. I now have greater confidence to tackle situations that I previously would have dreaded. Despite the often stressful environment within which I work, I have found it easier to relax and am far more effective as a result.'
Andy Nibloe, Director, Heath Lambert Consulting Limited

'Fiona is a remarkable person. Her warmth, drive and self-confidence are inspirational.'
Sarah Bradshaw, investment banker

The 10-Minute Life Coach

Fast-working Strategies for a Brand New You

Fiona Harrold

HODDER

MOBIUS

Hodder & Stoughton

First published in Great Britain in 2002 by Hodder and Stoughton
A division of Hodder Headline

7 9 10 8

A CIP catalogue record for this title is available
from the British Library

ISBN 0 340 82201 5

Typeset in Bembo by Palimpsest Book Production Limited,
Polmont Stirlingshire
Printed and bound in Great Britain by
Mackays of Chatham plc, Chatham, Kent

Hodder and Stoughton
A division of Hodder Headline
338 Euston Road
London NW1 3BH

For my darling dad, Michael,
and my son, Jamie.

Acknowledgements

Thank you to a fabulous team at Hodder & Stoughton, Rowena Webb at the helm, assisted brilliantly by the Misses Emma Heyworth-Dunn and Caro Ness. Heartfelt thanks to the wonderful writer Deborah Bosley for just the right push at the beginning and to Lennox Morrison, Ian McCurrach and Jamie Kerr for consistent cheering throughout, the best friends a girl could have.

Thanks to my agent, Maggie Pearlstine, for all her enthusiasm and sheer cleverness. And, thanks to all of you fabulous Get-up-and-Go people who have taken the time and generosity to write and spur me on with your inspiring messages and news. You know who you are. Thank you.

Fiona Harrold

Contents

1

Life is Precious

Before I begin I want to ask you why you have picked up this book. What attracted you to it? What do you want from it? What difference can I make to your life? What difference do you want me to make? Most importantly, what difference do *you* want to make to your life? Don't for a moment think that you just want a good read. There are novels for that. No, the simple truth is that you want to enhance your life. You want to upgrade your lot. You want more of some things and less of others.

Certain breeds of human being are ever curious to refine themselves or their life that bit more. You are of this breed. I recognize you because I too am of that breed. And so are all my clients. From now on I will view you as an esteemed client – someone whom I admire and respect enormously because you have certain traits and characteristics that I value and find immensely attractive. You are my type of person. You are the type of person who quite simply wants to make the most of yourself and your life and be the best that you can possibly be. You are like a sponge, eager to absorb as much as you can from a book such as this to add value to yourself and your life and move up a notch or two. Above all, a dreary life is not for you. Whatever it takes, whatever the cost, you will not and could not settle for a dull, half-lived life. You will not shirk from the challenge of doing whatever it takes to be the person you really want to be and live the life you know you should be living. Giving up and giving in is just not an option. For you know that the very pursuit of your dreams makes life immediately more interesting. You have fun trying!

You already are this bright, shiny person. I certainly can't make you something or someone that you aren't already. But I can definitely make you make more of yourself. My talent is to make sure that you appreciate who you already are and that you live a life worthy of yourself. I do this with my clients, many of whom you'll be reading about in the pages to come, and I'll be doing it with you as well. By the end of this book and our journey together I want you to feel at least three inches taller than you are right now and to have developed some really tough muscles. Your backbone will be thicker and you will feel you have the guts for anything life throws at you. You are this person already. I just want you to notice and flex those muscles and attributes some more. And the more you use them the better shape you'll be in. I sometimes illustrate this to a client by suggesting that they think of themselves as wearing a fabulous designer suit, a Versace, Armani or Donna Karan, a terrific cut with superb fabric. Yet the suit is a size or two too big and hangs off them somewhat. I want you to rise up to your full height, develop those muscles and fill that suit.

We are about to embark on a journey together to make your life even better than it is right now. Together we will take your life to the next level for you, whatever that looks like. There doesn't even have to be anything really wrong with your life to want to make some changes and run an MOT on it. Even Plato – over 2000 years ago – knew that an un-examined life is an unlived life. I've yet to meet anyone, man, woman or child, who didn't want to bring something new and fresh into their lives. I'll always remember watching entrepreneur Richard Branson take part in the BBC programme, *Question Time* when he was bidding to run the National Lottery. One suspicious member of the audience asked him why he wanted to take over the lottery. Didn't he have enough to do, she said, running Virgin airlines, Virgin railways, Virgin banking, and surely, she said, he didn't need any more money, being a millionaire many times over, so why couldn't he just retire to his private island and relax? After a measured pause he spoke very slowly and said that he of course didn't need to do another day's work in his life and as he was planning to turn all lottery profits over to charities, he wouldn't make any money whatsoever if his bid was successful. He explained that strange though it may sound he simply wanted to run the lottery because he could do a lot of good with it. That in itself would give him immense satisfaction and he just wasn't the type of person to sit around and do nothing. Neither are you. Even if you fantasize about having the finances of a Richard Branson, you would still itch to do something interesting. *After your big break you'd want to get back into life again.* I observed this at close quarters with my own brother Brian just recently. Brian has enjoyed tremendous success in his business life and was able to retire from full-time work in his forties. After a well-earned year's break touring Spain's finest golf courses, he got the itch to do something else. He said he had no further challenges left in the commercial world and he had all the cars and houses he could ever wish for. He is now planning to volunteer his skills and a year's worth of his time to a charity in a developing country. Interesting people don't give up on life, they just find something new, worthwhile and fun to do!

The point is, there doesn't have to be anything 'wrong' with you to want to run a check and make sure your current life is still the one you should be living. Like all living things, it might be, or parts might be past their sell-by date. You could have outgrown your suit! If it's straining at the seams you might need to move on to a bigger one.

As we embark on this journey together I will act as your personal coach. My job is to coax, cajole, persuade and sometimes push you to be the best that you can be, to live the most meaningful, worthwhile, fun and satisfying life possible. I want to wake you up to the importance of living the best life possible for you. As we work together I want you to take this opportunity to stretch yourself more than you would otherwise. Don't worry about what this will look like right now as you'll have plenty of opportunities to figure that out soon. As your coach I will do everything in my power to assist your performance. With my support behind you, you will feel able to push and stretch yourself further than if you were on your own. I want you to take yourself more seriously and life a little less. I want you to appreciate how precious life is without being precious about it. Above all, don't tiptoe around it. Honour it, and yourself, by giving it everything you've got. I never cease to be amazed at how some people wander through their lives with no real conviction or appetite for it. They appear to sleepwalk through weeks and months of time without ever shaking themselves awake to full alertness. They also fail to appreciate how privileged we all are to live here in a developed nation with the freedom and opportunities to do and be anything we want. They also seem to assume that life goes on for ever. Let's remind ourselves of the facts. If we live to the age of seventy we have 840 months available to us. At thirty-five, we have 420 left. Take out a third for sleeping and you're left with 280 months available to you. Do your own sums and you'll get the picture. Of course I fully intend to live way beyond seventy, as you do, but it would be foolish not to grasp just how precious, and precarious life really is.

Thankfully you're not one of those people. How do I know this? Because you're here with me now. Believe me, if you were one of the 'sleepwalkers', you'd have left by now. Sometimes people are woken up by a shocking, life-threatening event, to emerge changed for evermore. When Heather Mills, who became Lady McCartney since her marriage to Paul, was seriously injured in a road accident, losing her left leg, she came back to life with greater clarity, conviction and passion than ever before. 'Having come so close to death I believe in making the most of the moment. I don't sit and question things. If you're not happy and you can't work it through, you get out.' You could call this impatience. I see it as a sharp appreciation of how short our time here is. To spend great chunks of it getting by, putting the time in, clock-watching, wishing time away, is a waste. You don't ever want to get to the point at seventy or eighty or earlier and think, what was it all about, what was it all for? Question everything. Regret nothing.

Don't wait for a wake-up call. It might not come. Far better to wake yourself up. Sit up and take a fresh look at yourself and what you're doing. Our mission is to ensure you're living the best life possible for you, right here, right now. No regrets, no tears. Just one fabulous life. Who wants to be average? Certainly not you. You aspire to be the best. You'll do what it takes because that's who you are, that's what you're made of. You'll take your chances, a few risks, the lows with the highs. It's all part of the hand you've been dealt. You'll work with what you've got. You already know there are are only two things that are certain in life, apart from death and taxes. They're change and uncertainty. Being happy with both, you're the master of your fate, the captain of your soul. The objective is a lived life. So, stay with me. Over the days and weeks ahead I invite you to use this book as your secret ally.

Begin at the beginning and work your way through, section by section, or just dip in anywhere at all. It is important, however to take a little time *every day*. Build yourself up and stay strong by taking as little as ten minutes a day to feed yourself in this way. At the end of each chapter you'll find a set of exercises. Find the time to do them, ten minutes will do. You can snatch this time from your day any time, any place, on the bus, on the way to work, over a coffee. I promise you that this little bit of input will stay with you and uplift your day. It will be ten minutes well spent. This continuous drip-drip effect will work through you, keeping you positive, uplifted and focused on a daily basis, little and often.

I've written *The 10-Minute Life Coach* in response to the hundreds of you who have written to me after reading my first book, *Be Your Own Life Coach*. The letters and e-mails I've received all tell of terrific changes that you have made in your lives, from leaving a job or relationship that had died to moving to another country and starting over. There were also countless testaments to vast surges of confidence and personal power. All of your stories were incredibly impressive. Many were moving and inspiring. Some of them can be found on my website.

As requested, here is the follow-up. *The Ten-Minute Life Coach* is the daily tonic that you asked for, to boost you, keep you strong and help you stay on track. Over the days and weeks ahead you're going to get stronger and cultivate profound self-esteem, enduring self-belief and self-confidence. You'll banish fear of failure once and for all, setting you free to take more risks. You will discover your unique life purpose using simple and practical techniques. Day by day you'll build a vast inner charge of positive energy and personal power, finding it easier to draw the right people to you. You will redefine yourself; you will unlabel yourself. You'll get 'on-side', *your* side – and never knowingly undersell or short-change yourself again. You will learn how to get behind yourself, ridding yourself of the fear and anxiety that so many people carry, to build internal poise and power. You will develop a charisma that comes from the self-assuredness and self-possession that you have within. Above all, you'll take decisive action so that you can live on the edge of your potential. You're going to bring out the very best in yourself, making your mark, so you're in no doubt that you're living the fullest life for you – the best possible life.

It will show in your face. You'll look well, rested, freshened up, full of life. Come on. There's no time to lose.

Life is precious.

2

Stand Tall

I want you to begin to think about growing taller, rising up to your full height, stretching and expanding to grow into yourself. If you want a bigger life, if you want to expand your existing one, you first of all have to grow bigger yourself. You don't have to be someone else, just your true, fully fledged, perfectly brilliant self.

I want you to see yourself clearly, through a fresh pair of eyes. I want you to notice who you really are. I want you to see yourself as I would see you if I was working with you personally. Let me explain.

Rachel came to see me, saying that she wanted to be more effective at work and have more of a life outside the office. When I read through the information she sent to me on her life to date I was deeply impressed and full of admiration for her. I also knew at once that she was oblivious to the incredible person that she truly was.

Rachel was a real high-flyer, a 36-year-old City lawyer with a six-figure salary and a flat in London's Chelsea. She was exceptionally clever, having been a straight 'A' student and the first girl from her school to get a place at Oxford University. Why, you might be thinking, would she be coming to see me? I was thinking the same thing myself! Then I suddenly realized: Rachel didn't appreciate who she was. She didn't see herself the way I did and took no pleasure in her achievements. As she talked during our first session I understood why.

First of all, Rachel did not perceive herself to be particularly bright. She had never really taken the time to notice. She had simply clocked up result after result and carried on to the next challenge. At school she had 'kept her head down' and just got on with the job of studying and doing well. She was bullied mercilessly and the years of stress took so great a toll that her hair began to fall out. It was particularly bad when the exam results were announced when, as usual, she shone. But Rachel knew that she was about to suffer at the very moment of her success. She had to literally 'watch her back' and 'keep a low profile'. She was loathed and isolated because of her brilliance. Ironically, during our session, which was over the phone, I had a very clear impression of Rachel stooping and literally keeping her head down, as though she were so much taller than everyone else around her and compensating for her stature. When I mentioned this to her and asked if she felt physically bigger than her work colleagues, she agreed instantly and said that her posture was noticeably marked and her neck and shoulders regularly ached. At five foot ten inches, she felt that she towered over people. She was literally bringing herself down to their level. How much better it would be for them to stretch and reach up to her level, I said, only half joking! The other reason that Rachel kept herself small was that she had been brought up to do so. Her father was a Methodist minister and humility would have been an unspoken code of conduct in their household. Drawing any attention to one's talent, however God-given, would not have been encouraged. Doing well would have been expected, not celebrated. So, the overwhelming message Rachel would have learned about herself and life was that she mustn't upset others and that she must contain, even reduce herself, to avoid standing out and making others feel small.

It was incredibly important for Rachel to piece all of this together herself. More importantly, as an adult she could now choose to alter her behaviour, her attitude and the entire course of her life as a result. My programme with Rachel had one overriding objective – to support her to rise up to her full height and be the fabulous, powerful person she really was. It was now safe for her to be successful. She might still have the scars from her past, literally, but she no longer needed to cower before anyone. Rachel was ready to stand tall.

One of the first exercises I asked Rachel to do was to begin to see herself as I had when I saw her life on paper for the first time, when my response was *omigod*! I asked her to make a list with the heading, 'Reasons to see myself as exceptional'. I asked her to sit back, take a deep breath and have a look at her life. She presented me with ten convincing reasons. I was impressed. Was she? She was beginning to be. I had to talk her through each reason and point out the implication of it. For example, the fact that she had severe glandular fever when she sat her final exams at Oxford and *still* secured a superb degree and that she became a partner in a City law firm after only twelve months. Gradually I coaxed her to see her achieve-ments. Above all, she had never given in or given up. All those years ago she had taken the decision to stand up to the bullies and do her best in those exams year after awful year. She had refused to reduce herself and took the consequences.

Three months later Rachel had grown into herself. Without being in any way belligerent she had asserted herself as a major player at work, exuded poise and capability, and was offered the top job in the company. Did this create a little tension, a few raised eyebrows? Definitely. But it was not a problem.

Rachel simply carried on being herself, neither apologizing nor explaining away her promotion.

Now back to you. Just how tall are you? Do you keep yourself small to fit in? Do you think you're brilliant? If not, why not? Are you proud of yourself and your life? Are you aware of your finest moments? Are you perhaps thinking right now that you aren't in the same league as Rachel? If you think you have room to grow, if you'd like to grow and fill out a bit, then stay with me. If you feel that you probably don't see yourself in a good light, read on.

Successful high achievers are not necessarily embraced in British culture. Standing out – lifting your head above the parapet – can make you feel inclined to stoop, to keep your head down. The British are very ambiguous about success. Sometimes we seem beset with envy. Remember how everyone used to adore TV chef Jamie Oliver? Now it's fashionable to hate him, for his books, his TV series, his adverts, his model wife, his success. Oh how we loved it when EMI paid Mariah Carey *not* to sing. J.K. Rowling is about to get the same treatment. One tabloid newspaper has already started by accusing her unfairly of enjoying her new-found success as the world's wealthiest author too much to complete the latest Harry Potter book. 'Friends' have been quoted as saying how much she's changed now she's a celebrity. No wonder successful people in Britain often escape to the US before they become hate figures here. Americans like success because it was the search for prosperity and well-being – the immigrant experience – that took them all there in the first place.

The use of scapegoats is as old as civilization itself – examples of it can be found in cultures all around the world. The practice lives on today. Burning more brightly than those around you attracts attention and unnerves the insecure. At the same time society craves larger-than-life figures, people who stand above the general throng. Never be afraid of the qualities that set you apart. Don't consider shrinking to fit in with others. Don't court others' acceptance. Rise up to your full height. Swell out and take up your due space. Beware the 'imposter syndrome' where people wait to be found out and exposed as being not up to the job. This is incredibly common and is utterly disastrous for your morale and ability to perform at your best. Whether you're the CEO or it's your first day, don't ever short-change yourself in your own self-appraisal. Don't fall short. You're up to it! Hike yourself up the extra few inches! Success doesn't thrive on self-doubt. Whether you're running the show or planning to, what's required is confidence, courage and the ability not to give a damn about what your audience thinks of you. This is particularly key if you're female.

Females are more modest than men – research proves it – and it gets them nowhere at work. A study at Edinburgh University has discovered that men tend to overestimate their abilities while women are inclined to think too little of themselves. The research, which probed the intellectual self-image of 502 women and 265 men, revealed that men consistently rated their own IQs seven points higher than women. When these beliefs were rated against actual performance, the women turned out to be right, while the men had delusions of intellectual grandeur. Coyness and modesty can have no place on the CV of the modern working woman. Women in Britain are being paid less than men because they are perceived as willing to accept less. Sara Solnick, Assistant Professor of Economics at Vermont University, published her findings recently in the journal, *Economic Inquiry*. 'Women consistently earn less than men, are quoted higher prices for cars and gain smaller increases in salary when they choose to bargain,' she said. The Equal Opportunities Commission agrees. They said, 'The expectation that women will settle for less could certainly be a factor in the earnings gap.'

Obviously, you're not in the business of short-changing yourself. Standing tall and standing up for yourself aren't about being obnoxious. They're about being authentic, true and straightforward. They're about being effective in your expression, knowing your worth and valuing yourself appropriately – taking a stand when necessary, walking away on occasions. Fitting in so you don't stand out is not something to aspire to, whatever you've been told. And don't for a moment think that being powerful isn't sexy. It's the greatest aphrodisiac. Wear it well. Don't let it hang off you. Make it fit. Get comfortable with your own power. Gel with it. Embody it.

Madonna was in the news recently when she fired a security guard after arriving at her home to find that he seemed to have disappeared for lunch – with the only set of keys. Well, good for her, I say. We need some forthright American females to show us that it's OK to be authoritarian when people are not doing what they are paid to do. This security guard was probably more used to working for polite British clients who would rather do anything than stand up for themselves. Any woman who throws her weight around is often judged negatively. Don't let that put you off. If you don't stick up for yourself your life can swiftly spin out of control. I frequently see people who could be twice as good as they already are. In themselves, in their professional life, in their social and personal life. The shortfall comes from how they're looking at themselves, what they don't see. Thankfully this won't be the case with you. It's only when you're at the full height of your personal power that you know what you're made of and what you're capable of. Pull yourself up. Don't be coy.

STAND TALL

1. *Get you!*

Do you? Do you see yourself clearly or are you in the habit of denying your worth and talents even to yourself? Deny them long enough and they'll slip over the horizon altogether. Look to the past, just for a moment, and pinpoint whether staying small was seen as a virtue. Were you taught to keep your head down? Get clear.

2. *You are exceptional.*

If *you* say so. You have good reasons to see yourself as gifted and exceptional. Notice them. Make a list, 'Reasons why I know I'm exceptional'. Keep this list open until you have at least twenty compelling, convincing reasons. They're there. You might just need to note them down for yourself. Keep this list around as a handy reminder.

3. *Success breeds success*

– but only if you appreciate that success in the first place. Then you have a valuable asset tucked away that you know you can tap into any time you like and use to generate more of the same. No one can diminish it or take it away from you. Today and occasionally thereafter, polish that asset. Do an inventory. Compile a list: 'Successes in my life that I'm truly thrilled with'. Go way back. You've been achieving for a long time. Be expansive in notching up your triumphs. Success is personal. See yourself as a successful *person*, not merely a good worker. Nothing succeeds quite like success. Make yours work for you.

4. *Say no.*

Get good and entirely comfortable about saying no. Have a variety of phrases that you've already prepared that all spell you setting boundaries for yourself. This isn't about being a monster. It's about acting like a grown-up and having a say in your life. It's about

14

getting a grip and treating yourself with some respect. And you know what they say – if you don't, no one else will. It's true.

5. Walk tall.
Don't slump. Hold yourself with pride. Carry yourself with a sense of purpose. Stride out. You're going places. Look lively. If you're in the habit of slouching, work on your posture with some Alexander Technique lessons or any other physical therapy. Don't let your body let you down. Shoulders down and back. Neck relaxed. Eyes ahead. Don't look down. Best foot forward.

Life is short. It's also too darned long to live a life that's just too small or that you've grown out of. Better to have a life with some room for you to grow. You can have a growth spurt at any age. At some point today, drink a toast to you! Embrace yourself. Think yourself lucky. Seeing yourself as you do, you wouldn't want to be anyone else. Celebrate yourself. Smile. Swell with pride. Stretch and grow. You're looking good!

Stand tall.

3

Believe and Conquer

I'm no football fanatic but I'll never forget the match between England and Argentina in the 2002 World Cup tournament. Even I could see that they were playing an incredible game to beat Argentina 1–0. More than half the country watched and wondered how the England team had transformed themselves in the course of seven days. A week earlier we had watched and groaned as they played a limp game against Sweden, drawing 1–1. This was the same team, but they were now in a different league from a week ago. What made the difference? How could the same players be so very different? They were all as super-fit as they had been a week ago. Performance enhancing drugs are banned, so what happened?

England's secret weapon was a quietly spoken Norwegian sports psychologist who talked David Beckham and his team-mates out of despair before their thrilling victory. Dr Willi Railo inspired key players to believe that they could win the match and then the World Cup itself. Railo had hastily arranged personal coaching calls to several of the England's stars after their dismal performance with Sweden had left the players dejected. 'I spoke to some England players before the Argentina game about self-confidence and self-belief and the need to dare to lose a match in order to win it,' said Railo. The conversations helped to convince the players, especially Beckham, the captain, that they could beat their old enemies and they passed on that positive message to their team-mates. The pep talks gave England the psychological edge before kick-off. Railo told the players they had to risk losing if they were to triumph. 'Winners hate to lose,' he said, 'but winners aren't afraid of losing. And winners dare to win.'

This is a recipe for winning at anything in life, from personal relationships and the state of your health to success in the workplace. The willingness to dare to win while not being afraid of losing is at the very heart of indestructible self-belief. Fear of failure curbs the kind of risk-taking that often leads to success. 'When I'm working with players it's to mentally strengthen them to be more confident, to realize their full potential, to help them believe they can win the World Cup, to take away mental blocks and teach them to be able to win under stress,' Railo said.

Self-belief is your secret ally. You've just got to be able to turn it on, to boost it when you need it most. It's part of the armoury of all people who achieve great things. To win at anything in life, your greatest battle is with yourself. Your most powerful enemy is within. Your greatest ally is there also. The person who has the weapon to make you win or lose is *you*. Your weapon is your mind. Your mental approach makes you strong or weak, tough or flabby. Conquering yourself is the ultimate challenge. Great self-believers have the edge. They carry within a formidable advantage over the average person. They know how to dig deep and muster additional resources and back-up when necessary. They never lose. They always live to fight another day. They always come through. Even if you identify yourself as one of the great self-believers, you'll still be eager to run a check on your current levels to ensure you're in peak condition.

Colossal, all-conquering self-belief is not confined to sport. It's something our heroes of today share with heroes of old. Take, for example, Alexander the Great. From the age of twenty until his death at thirty-three, he led his handful of elite fighters from the then disregarded kingdom of Macedonia to conquer Persia, Egypt, Babylon and swathes of India and the Middle East. Huge armies and empires fell before his tiny band, driven on only by the power of his self-belief and insane courage. His power and magnetism subdued the whole world known to him. Consider Napoleon, a mere corporal from Corsica, who by dint of personality took hold of what was left of the French army, a rabble besieged on all sides. But under Napoleon, that same army conquered and controlled the rest of Europe for fifteen years.

Alexander, Napoleon and people like them, such as Caesar and Churchill, altered the course of history. Their dreams may not necessarily have been good but, good or bad, these are the people who change the world. Margaret Thatcher, Britain's only female Prime Minister, ran her party, Parliament and the country with an iron grip. Not for nothing was she known as the Iron Maiden. She achieved her goals through her sheer self-belief. As, in other ways and in other contexts, did Gandhi, St Francis of Assisi, Joan of Arc and Martin Luther King. What all these figures had in common was a degree of self-belief that allowed them to achieve what lesser, more cautious mortals would have regarded as impossible and unrealistic. Those with the self-belief of a Mrs Thatcher, or an Alexander, or a pumped-up David Beckham can think the unthinkable because they are not constrained by what others think possible. Their self-belief, focused and honed as it is, gives them an insight and a breadth of vision lacking in the average person.

Great self-believers have an uncanny knack of pushing aside obstacles to their dream. To ordinary mortals they can appear obsessive in the pursuit of their goals, driving on and on long after the rest of us would have retired or given up. But unlike

ordinary mortals, they do go on and they win. These are the
people who change minds, and who live life to the full. These
are the people who do what others cannot dare even to dream.
The world is certainly richer and more fascinating for them
for they know better than anyone what can be done if we
really believe in ourselves.

Are great self-believers made or born? Can anyone be one?
There can be no doubt that having self-belief instilled in you
from an early age is a huge advantage. Having a parent or
authority figure implant and nurture your self-belief as you are
still forming – so that it becomes woven into the very fabric
of your being – builds a phenomenal powerhouse. Major new
research shows this conclusively.

Richard Branson and Cherie Blair were destined to be
successful from the age of ten. Both had significant emotional
support from an early age, enjoying high levels of self-esteem
and self-belief. This, more than any other factor, is what gave
them the edge. 'There is now clear evidence that children with
higher self-esteem at 10 get as much of a kick to their adult
earning power as those with higher maths or reading ability,'
said Leon Feinstein of the influential Centre for Economic
Performance at the London School of Economics, which carried
out the study. The effects of academic disadvantage or social
deprivation can both be overcome with self-belief. The Virgin
entrepreneur Richard Branson left school at sixteen with
mediocre qualifications and was also dyslexic. However, he came
from an affluent and supportive upper middle-class family – his
mother and grandmother were both famously supportive. He
went on to become one of the twenty richest men in Britain.
Cherie Blair grew up in a relatively poor family with little
academic background but had significant support from her
mother Gale. She is now one of Britain's most distinguished

barristers, reportedly earning £250,000 a year. British society is filled with highly successful people who underperformed at school but, boosted by self-confidence from an early age, have become successful in their chosen careers. Max Clifford, now one of Britain's leading publicists, says, 'If you're brought up with self-esteem you're happy to take a risk, you don't dread the consequences of making mistakes, and that leads to success . . . I was taught to believe I was as good as anyone else.'

Schools are geared to helping pupils achieve good exam scores. They are not institutions created to help individual children achieve their psychological growth. You may not have received the best possible psychological input as you were growing up – no matter – all the more incentive to make up for it now. The truth is that you can grow your own self-belief any time you decide to do so. I am going to act as your coach in this regard. Awareness is 50 per cent of the battle. Waking up to the need for greater self-belief, alerting yourself to its power, takes you to the halfway line. Thereafter I'm going to provide you with a winning formula that you can follow for your own victories. Before I do that I want to tell you about someone I met who demonstrated the rare, indestructible breed of self-belief that I want for you, *in spite of* the influence of her school.

Anne McKevitt is just about to take the US by storm as their new lifestyle queen, the new Martha Stewart. Designer Anne is poised to clinch a deal with a US TV network, which is rumoured will earn her in the region of £25 million. Yet Anne has no formal training in interior design, having left school three months before her sixteenth birthday. Home was a two-bedroom council house in the far north of Scotland and school was an ordeal: 'I loathed school. I just felt I was being held back all the time . . . I remember the headmaster saying he thought I was making a terrible mistake [to leave] and I told him that I'd prove him wrong.'

When I met Anne a few years ago she was part of the popular BBC home make-over programme, *Home Front*. An observer might have said she was the least likely of the team to make a successful US leap. She was new to television and her broad Scots accent was a challenge for British viewers, never mind our US cousins. I needed no more than five minutes in her company to see that her mental approach made her success a certainty. She had unshakeable belief in herself. Whatever life threw at her she'd handle. She'd just keep on going, in spite of setbacks or obstacles. The bigger the problem, the bigger she'd become. She clearly had a desire to be as big as she could be, to take herself to the wire, to the very edge of her potential. And she believed utterly in her flair for design and her ability to take the world by storm. She was invincible, her self-belief indestructible. When I read about her US success recently in the newspapers I wasn't in the least surprised.

How much do you believe in yourself? How much do you show faith, give yourself opportunities, breaks, chances? Are you your own worst enemy or your greatest ally? Are you on-side? Can you be relied on to stand firm when the going gets tough, to keep up your support, to back yourself all the way? Ask yourself this: 'What difference would it bring to my life if I doubled my self-belief?' Excited? You should be.

How big could you be? As big as you want to be. What do you need to get there? *You need shedloads of self-belief.* You need to be your very own personal self-belief generator, churning out as much as you need; a constant flow for everyday life, speeding up to produce vast amounts more on occasion. A limitless supply of self-belief, on demand. When do you want it? NOW!

BELIEVE AND CONQUER

1. *Become a believer.*
Decide right now to join the ranks of the great self-believers. Tell no one. This is your secret. This means that you think, speak and act as a believer. Have total self-belief. Do not for one moment think that you can't achieve your goal. Winning requires flexibility, vigilance and sometimes a change of tactics and strategy, but that's all part of the game. Don't countenance failure – get it out of the equation. Prepare to win. Plan a strategy for success. Think about every step along the path. Order the stages in sequence until you reach it.

2. *Kickstart your powerhouse.*
Your stores of self-belief are within. They're limitless. You have an endless, self-generating supply. It doesn't matter whether the wheels are a little sluggish. The machinery is still intact. Use it. Get it going. Pump it up. Fuel it with your urge to change some aspect of your life, attitude, or behaviour. Feed it with your desire. Know that the single most important distinction between winners and losers is the degree of self-belief each summons up. Just keep on producing more and more self-belief as the situation demands. Have courage. Dig deep. There's absolutely no shortage.

3. *Take responsibility for yourself.*
Don't ever look back and wallow. It's a precious waste of your focus. You are in charge now. Think like a winner. You're a self-styled self-believer now, of your own design, by choice. You know your most powerful weapon is your mental approach and you use it well. You appreciate its power to set you up to win or lose. It's your ultimate tool. You respect its influence to make or break. You keep it sharp and polished. You look after it well and it serves you well. Look forward with optimism.

4. *Think big.*

Believe that anything is attainable. Play a bigger game. Bite off more than you think you can chew – then watch yourself rise to the occasion. Galvanize yourself for the big push, the extra mile you'll need to go. You'll be surprised how quickly you achieve results. Remember the sky is the limit if you have self-belief and focus on the outcome. Go beyond what you think you can do. Play to win.

5. *Borrow or buy in additional self-belief.*

If your own stores are running low and you need a boost, don't hesitate to use an outside supply to charge yours. High achievers in all areas of life use coaches and outside trainers to strengthen themselves. It's not a sign of weakness. It's another one of your tools to keep you strong. It's a transfusion straight to your own storehouse to boost your own supply. Only work with someone who sees your potential – if they don't get you, they won't make you stronger. They have to believe in you utterly and admire your potential. You have to believe in them.

Choose to believe. Show faith. Stoke up that furnace, your powerhouse of self-belief. Keep it burning away and when you need a boost, dig into your supply. It's there to be used. Ignore it and it'll get out of condition. You need never go short or run out. You've got a limitless supply. The more you generate, the more you have at your disposal. There's no one and nothing in your way. Pump it up. Work it. Build unshakeable self-belief. Remember: Play to win. Dare to lose. Go for it.

Onwards and upwards.

Believe and conquer.

4

Love You

When the going gets tough and the pressure is on, it's not necessarily the talented ones who rise to the challenge. It's the ones who love themselves. 'Narcissists rush in where angels fear to tread. They may not be highly talented, but they believe in themselves, don't fear failure and respond brilliantly to pressure. It is often called self-love, but it can be very useful,' Dr Roy Baumeister of the Case Western Reserve University in Ohio told the British Psychological Society earlier this year. He arrived at this conclusion from the results of his study of 248 undergraduates.

Do you love you? Do you really like yourself? It's a simple enough question. The correct answer is, 'Yes, I do actually.' 'Maybe' just won't do. A moment or two is all it takes to reflect and feel a resounding 'Yes' well up inside you. If this isn't the case, don't worry, you're not alone! In fact, I'd be surprised if you were a positive 'Yes', simply because so few people are, and I ask this question a lot; it's part of my job.

A large part of what I am employed by people to do is to guide them to be the best that they can be, to live their best possible life, to live a great life. And I tell you now that liking yourself and feeling you deserve this great life is absolutely fundamental to your success. In fact, you could even be living your great life, but because you don't like yourself enough, you'll feel unable to enjoy it and make the most of it. That's a nice problem to have, you might be thinking, but actually all the riches on earth can't buy you a good feeling about yourself. I know this because I've worked closely with people in this very situation; people who have squillions in the bank and a queasiness in their stomachs. Believe me, you are far better off if you possess a good, clean, healthy feeling about yourself; if you take a pride in who you are and feel delighted and grateful to be *you*. In this case, you are the one who is advantaged, living a privileged life, the good life. This is what I want for you. I want this for you for two reasons; first, the more you see yourself as a good person, the more powerful you become and the more you are a force for good in the world. And the world needs good people. Second, good people deserve to live their best possible life. They just do. They've earned it.

Good people are the most likely to dislike themselves. The reason for this is that they desire to do good. They feel compelled to be good, to do the right thing, to cause no harm or suffering to another living being. This might sound a little pious, but that's how it is, and I suspect that you might be recognizing yourself here. And the reason they are most likely to dislike themselves is simply this – good people are always the most sensitive, thin-skinned and open to suggestion. This is acutely the case when they are children and at their most vulnerable. Their tendency to blame themselves for anything and everything that goes wrong in their world and the world at large takes root here.

As a child you don't have the sophistication to reason and save yourself from being damaged by the circumstances and events of your life. Your sense of who you are is overwhelmingly shaped by the individuals around you. You believe what you're told to believe by the authority figures in your life. And, when you're a child, there is no easy escape route. You're trapped in that environment, however gruesome it might be. If you were really lucky, then you'll have absorbed high-quality messages and beliefs about yourself, because your authority figures were outstanding people who appreciated the power they had to shape your identity. In my experience, this situation is exceptional. Parents and teachers are only now really grasping the profound and far-reaching impact of their words and messages on young minds. There's a long way to go. Look around you and listen for the damage being done even now, the seeds of self-loathing and guilt being sown in impressionable young hearts and minds. Only the other day a twelve-year-old friend of my son Jamie was tormenting himself because he felt so stupid. This was the result of him being told by his teacher that unless he got all twenty of his answers correct in a maths test he was unlikely to get a decent job. Jamie's friend got seventeen correct and so he drew the conclusion suggested to him.

Parents can also be guilty of the most appalling neglect and ignorance when it comes to giving their own children the best start in life. And because, as children, you're in their company every day for the most impressionable years of your life, you invariably take their messaging to heart. You assume they know best about everything and so their words of insight and wisdom fall on very fertile ground. Whether they were right or wrong, wise or foolish, you tend to believe them. You assume they must be right about you. And our culture confirms this by putting people onto a pedestal once they join the ranks of 'parents'. We are told: 'Honour thy father and thy mother' without question or answering back.

So, is it any wonder that the most ingrained, irrational and stubborn messaging is usually from one or both parents? And the most bizarre thing is this: it is overwhelmingly the negative input that we hold onto and regard as true, whether from both parents or only one. You could have received completely different, conflicting messages from each.

I recently began working with Christine who, in her forties, still wasn't sure what to believe about herself and whether she liked herself or not. She was actually a fabulous person but it was her misfortune to have had a deeply unhappy, frustrated woman as a mother, who fed Christine the most transparent nonsense about not getting 'too big for her boots' or 'getting above anyone else'. On the other hand she had a father who loved her spirit, who saw that she was likely to lead a very different life from her mother. Christine's father adored her for the very same reasons that her mother resented her. How confusing is that for a nine year old? Christine had taken as truth her mother's thoughts and words about her. As a result she really didn't like herself very much. She felt unlikeable and a fake, as one of her mother's favourite sayings was that if people knew what she was *really* like they'd have nothing to do with her. Christine was effectively programmed to see herself as a bad, insincere person. This brainwashing became absolute with the death of Christine's adoring father when she was eleven.

The irony is that Christine did go on to live a fairytale life, complete with castle and a position in the world that was a lifetime away from her impoverished upbringing, exactly as her father had predicted. But she had never really felt comfortable with herself and even though she enjoyed incredible wealth, she never indulged herself with luxurious treats as you might expect. She was Lady Bountiful, generous to everyone and mean to herself. I worked with Christine intensively for three months to coach her to like herself. Thankfully, it worked. She has now chosen to believe her father's much healthier, truer thoughts and beliefs about her, and sees herself for the thoroughly good, decent person that she is.

Deep inside all of us, there is someone we were meant to be. But, too often, we define ourselves by our circumstances and feel great only if things are going well. If life goes badly, we feel worthless or look to other things or people or the 'perfect' job to define us and prop up our self-esteem. We discover our true identities by finding out what we want – and do not want – to do. You will have received a range of messages from your earliest days; some will be absolutely fine, some may even be incredibly powerful and useful. My interest here lies with the messages that may impair your vision of yourself, that clog up your ability to feel 'clean' about yourself. Unless you've conscientiously detoxed yourself, then assume with me that you have impacted waste material festering away in your psyche, the result of years upon years of accumulated junk messages absorbed by you from the outset. It has to go! In order for you to feel clean and wholesome, we have to root this out. The alternative is to live with chronic, low-level uncertainty about yourself, undermining your aliveness, your personal power and effectiveness in the world. Thankfully, this will not be the case for you.

LOVE *YOU*

1. *Love you.*
   Why not? If not you, then who? And why not? Aren't you loveable? Of course you are. You'd better believe it. You have to *see* it, otherwise you'll never feel truly good in your own skin. Right here, right now, make the decision to appreciate yourself more, give credit where it's due, talk yourself up. Cultivate kindness, compassion and

respect – for *you*. Face the truth. You came into this world on your own and you'll leave it on your own. At some point in between it makes sense to get comfortable with yourself. It's your life. At the end of it you'll answer to yourself – you'll hold yourself account-able so it's best to start doing it now. Don't ever demean or demor-alize yourself in public or private. Talk yourself up. Drop false modesty. Speak only well of yourself. Exude self-assurance.

2. *Change the record.*

Whose opinions, thoughts and beliefs are stuck in your mind? If they're not yours and they're of no value to you, don't hold onto them. You're a grown-up now. You can think your own thoughts. You can choose what to give room to. It doesn't matter how long some stuff has been there. If it's toxic, get rid of it.

Write down this statement: 'What I learned about myself from my mother/father was'. List all the main messages from each parent and asterisk the ones that leave you feeling uneasy about yourself. Repeat this with all the principal players of your upbringing. Enough is enough. Draw a line under the stuff that is clearly pure nonsense, spoken in heat, ignorance, spite or jealousy, but that has lodged with you. See it for what it is. Decide right now to stop giving a home to this garbage. Starve it of attention. Laugh at it. Stop taking it seriously. Only you know the truth. Only you get to decide what to believe about you. You're a work in progress. Write: 'I now choose to see myself as . . .' and make a list as long as you like. Be your-self. Be whoever you like. You decide. Then live it.

3. *Reasons to like yourself.*

Liking yourself is your birthright. Maintaining it requires momentum. Continually give yourself good reasons to like yourself. Remind your-self who you really are. Be everything you desire and admire in others, *yourself.* This requires right thinking *and* right action. Keep on acquiring more evidence to sustain your conviction. Right now, draw up a list, 'Reasons to like myself'; include character traits and specific actions you are proud of yourself for. Think about future actions that you can take to ensure this continued flow of good-will towards others and, thereby, yourself.

4. *Enjoy yourself.*

Come on, when was the last time you took yourself out for lunch, or did something special just for you? Spoil yourself. Spend some quality time with you. Wine and dine yourself. Think about you. What would be fun for you? Do you know how to enjoy yourself? Chill out with your new best friend – you! Discover your hidden depths, your likes and dislikes. What makes you tick? Get some strong opinions. Entertain yourself. If you don't find yourself good company, how can others? Treat yourself well, but above all, treat yourself.

5. *Look cared for.*

You'll give off a far better air about yourself. Pay attention to pres-entation. How looked after and cared for do you look? Grooming speaks volumes. Look immaculate. Smell divine. Wear great under-wear. Get 'the look'. Buy the sharpest haircut you can afford. Stay with it. Last season's must-have item was cutting-edge *then*. Appearances matter. Keep up. Don't look neglected. If you have no pride, nobody can give it to you.

Put the effort in. Find yourself attractive, likeable, loveable. Adorn yourself with the qualities and attributes you admire most. Wear them well. Make yourself downright irresistible. Judging by your own standards, you're fabulous, always compelling, immensely likeable, utterly loveable. Look at you.

Love you!

5

Be Good

No one can tell you what you should or shouldn't do. Integrity and character are of your own making. You won't be popular with some people – you can't please everyone all the time – but you can please yourself and create your own set of principles. Your own set of personal ethics or values will support your sense of self, your tone of mind, and will colour your entire experience of life. You may already be a dedicated follower of a particular religion, which underpins your daily life and behaviour. Nonetheless, as a freethinker you'll want to ensure that any doctrine you follow preaches values that you can wholeheartedly uphold.

For increasing numbers of us, organized religion has simply ceased to fulfil our spiritual needs. Church attendance is at an all-time low. Mainstream churches are struggling to attract worshippers but that doesn't mean that we're not exploring our spiritual side or that the need for organized religion and ritual has disappeared. In the immediate aftermath of the death of Diana, Princess of Wales, church attendance throughout the world soared. It's just that the Church is no longer providing the modern moral and spiritual leadership for many of us that it did for our parents' generation.

Additionally, religious fervour cannot be relied upon to bring out the best in human nature and promote tolerance and goodwill. Having grown up in Northern Ireland where religious rivalry divides neighbour from neighbour, leading to the deaths of thousands of innocent people, I've seen this first hand. Often it was the very religious leaders themselves who preached bigotry and hatred from their pulpits. My own philosophy nonetheless remains resolutely optimistic. I share with Rousseau the belief that the vast majority of us are born good and gifted in one way or another and need only to be fed and watered for this to grow. Even with the decline of religion, human beings still feel the need to live a good life, underpinned with a strong moral foundation, to experience themselves as good.

There has never been a more urgent time for us all to take responsibility for our own moral code, a framework for life based on clearly defined principles and ethics.

Life used to be much simpler. We were taught the difference between right and wrong from our religious elders. For me, abiding by the Ten Commandments was all that was required to feel I was a good person living a good life. That was until I discovered freethinking. On a perfect spring day in my eighteenth year I stood on the steps of the University of Ulster, gazed up at a glorious expanse of blue sky and declared that I was going it alone. From now on I would think for myself. I wasn't giving up on God. I just needed a break from being preached at. No more received morality for me. I needed to find my own way, set my own values, abide by my own rules. If I sinned and strayed, it would be from my own laws. Punishment, penance and forgiveness would be administered by my own authority, me. With one sweep, I replaced faith in uniformed clerics with faith in myself to be the arbitrator of my own good behaviour. As faith in outside authorities and dogma breaks down we need to decide on an alternative ethical stance. You need to have values to call your own, to live by, to live up to.

A clearly thought-out, heartfelt value system will stand you in good stead throughout your life. Major decisions and changes will be more straightforward as you will have a code of reference on which to base those decisions. *You* will be more straightforward. You will be more defined, thought out and clear-cut as a person. You will be your own person, answerable to yourself. Your personal standards will require you to uphold them. When you stray from your path, you'll recommit and reaffirm your position. You will have your own written constitution to govern your actions. As a result, your personal integrity will soar, giving you a depth and a clarity that nothing else will.

Your personal value and moral goodness is the bedrock on which your self-worth and self-esteem will sit. This solid moral framework of values and ethics will underpin your character and support your decisions and actions. Without this clarity you won't be entirely convinced of your intrinsic goodness or feel qualified to respect and admire yourself. And having the highest regard for yourself is vital because *your opinion* of yourself is the one that really counts. Ensure you have the highest opinion of yourself, your self-respect depends on it.

I am often asked how I feel about increasing someone's self-esteem, rendering them more powerful versions of themselves. What if they're not entirely good people? Surely it is of no service to the world to boost the power of a morally dubious individual? Good question. My answer is this. I only work with people whom I view as essentially good. I have to feel I can take up their cause and run with it alongside them. I have to admire them, to wholeheartedly, unreservedly, want the best for them. Am I making a judgement here? Absolutely. Because for me to be the best possible coach for people I have to feel strongly that I can stand by them, shoulder to shoulder, and champion their corner. Every fibre of my being has to feel total congruence with their aims and ambitions. Would I be the best coach for an ambitious arms manufacturer or the CEO of the world's biggest tobacco company, eager to create a new market among eleven to fourteen year olds in Vietnam? I don't think so.

The point I'm making here is that for you to be powerful and unreservedly effective in *your* world, *the* world, you must feel 100 per cent committed to yourself, to the purity and rightness of your mission. You must see yourself as truly deserving. You must be able to admire yourself, to defend yourself when called to, to be your own backer. Your character must be above reproach, blemish-free and shining. You must be able to front up to criticism or disapproval and quickly reach your own conclusion.

This is no fanciful idea. The extent to which you feel less than deserving is the extent to which you will restrict your personal power, reduce your momentum and withhold vital support for yourself. If you view yourself as less than a thoroughly good person, entirely deserving of good fortune and success, then we need to clean this up immediately. You already have a code of conduct, an underlying map that directs your behaviour and shapes your perspective. You may never have paid much attention to this code before. It's probably so much a part of you that you simply take it for granted. Don't! Much of it will be received wisdom that you've just picked up from the mental atmosphere of your parents' home. Some will have been conscientiously passed on to you from your elders at home and school. And you will have already applied your mind to moral issues and arrived at your own conclusions before now. I'm simply suggesting that you do this even more, so that you have total choice and clarity on who you are and where you stand. In a moment I'll take you through a simple guide to identify your most important values. First, let me demonstrate the importance of knowing what they are.

Jennifer was in her early forties when she came to see me. Her greatest fear was that she was turning into her mother. And she was. More precisely, she had unwittingly soaked up her mother's critical and mean-spirited approach. She was desperate to arrest this tendency at once and for ever. She felt uneasy with herself, unclear as to what sort of person she really was. If she really was this type of person, then good she certainly wasn't. Feeling ambivalent about herself and her intrinsic value meant that there was a distinct lack of generosity in her attitude to herself. Her conversation was peppered with references to herself as being 'nothing special'. This was far from the truth. In her quest to be a better person she read self-help and personal growth books compulsively. Her self-improvement involved relentless hard work without respite or reward. She would never be good enough.

One of the first things I required Jennifer to do was to desist from reading any further self-improvement books, even mine! The answers to her quest lay not in a book but in a face-to-face conversation with herself, looking at the woman in the mirror she had become and the one she wanted to become. In place of her serious study I recommended relaxing on a chaise longue with a copy of *Vogue*, certainly nothing more worthy than *Vanity Fair*. In other words, she had to lighten up.

Then I pointed out the simple truth to Jennifer that she already was a good person. There was ample evidence in her life to vindicate her. Her desire to elevate her character and refine her sensibility was to be admired. Slowly she began to grasp this. The rest of her challenge required her to police her responses and attitudes so that she could engender the qualities and values she prized, generosity, openness and tolerance replacing criticism, meanness and bitterness. This was no easy task. Jennifer had been raised on a daily diet of negativity. Years of junk conditioning had left her feeling poisoned and warped. It would require continual vigilance to change those mental habits of a lifetime.

The good news for Jennifer and for you is that you are already good. To be reading this book, to be pursuing this line of enquiry within yourself is evidence that you *desire* to be and do good. The *desire* to be and do good is what distinguishes you from individuals who lack moral backbone. Trust me, it is only intrinsically decent people who put themselves under a probing spotlight and ask awkward questions about goodness, morality and the nature of a good life. People like you who are eager to better yourself, to make the best of yourself, to be the best, instinctively seek to improve your fundamental character. Indeed, it could be argued that refining and polishing our character so that when we pass on from this lifetime we are much-enhanced versions of our original state is the ultimate challenge for all of us. What higher pursuit can there be than that of being a better person? How else do you get to feel clean and pure within? How else can you stand on your own two feet and, when called to, defend your integrity without a strong moral foundation beneath you? Where does moral fibre come from if not from your own stock of clarity and integrity? And how else can you like yourself and feel you deserve the very best if you don't feel inherently good?

In the 1950s an American psychologist, Abraham Maslow, studied mature, successful and fulfilled people, and concluded that we could all be that way for it is our natural human state. Maslow coined the phrase 'hierarchy of need' to explain the psychology of human needs. Understandably, the most basic need is for food and water and we care for little else until that need is met. Once we have secured a supply of food and water, we begin to concern ourselves with items such as shelter, clothing and safety. Again, once these are in place, we begin to focus on our social needs, the need to belong to a grouping. These needs are met in part by our family, but also through joining clubs and associations. Next we seek to satisfy our desire for the esteem of others, by competing with them for power, victory or recognition. This extroverting need is eventually displaced by a subtler esteem need, the need for self-esteem. Here we demand higher standards of ourselves, and look to our own criteria to measure ourselves, rather than to how others see us.

Maslow's highest state was the self-actualizing person who emerges when both the esteem needs are satisfied and the individual is no longer driven by the need to prove themselves, either to themselves or to anyone else. He called this self-actualizing because self-actualized would imply that we could really arrive at that state, whereas he saw it as a never-ending journey. The need associated with self-actualizers is the need for meaning and purpose in their lives. They want their work, their activities and their existence to have some value, to be a contribution to others.

This is who *you* are. In ensuring that your own declared ethics and values are of the highest order, for your own good and the good of all concerned, you are stretching to live life at the most evolved, refined state that a human being can.

In addition, living in a society such as ours requires us to agree on some common values. The decline of religion has left a vacuum which, thankfully, governments and schools are now beginning to fill. From September 2002 schools in the UK will have introduced a citizenship course into the curriculum for all fifteen to eighteen-year-old students, with the express intention of helping young people develop a personal ethical position rather than one derived from parental, social or peer pressure. The first business ethics course has just been launched in the UK in secondary schools by the charity, Jewish Association for Business Ethics. Entitled 'money and morals', the course is designed to make students aware of the need in the workplace for 'honesty, integrity and social responsibility'.

Now, let's take a look at your personal ethical position (PEP).

BE GOOD

1. *Get with it.*
You're already 'good'. Your desire and your quest to be and do good demonstrates this. Refining and fine-tuning your desire is exemplary. Good for you.

2. *Get clear.*
Your values are qualities or characteristics that you're already drawn to. They're already part of your personal make-up. By identifying them overtly and declaring allegiance to them you strengthen their impact on your character and your life.

Right now, list your top ten values, in no particular order. Examples could include, honesty, generosity, fairness. Now choose your top four. These should shape your goals and actions, the entire course of your life. The crucial point to always bear in mind when asserting your values is this: make very sure that you cause no harm or suffering to any other person in the expression and pursuit of those values. Express yourself and your values for your own highest good and *the good of all concerned.*

3. *Be authentic.*
Another way to spot your values is to recall really important incidents in your life where you felt compelled to speak out or take

action, regardless of the consequences. Think of a few situations where you didn't speak out or act on your instinct. On reflection, do you wish you had? Do you sometimes feel uncomfortable with yourself as a result? Both scenarios give you vital information about the nature of right and wrong for you. Get clear what those specific values are. When you express them you are being true to yourself. To thine own self be true. This is the 'real' you.

4. *Demonstrate*.
To feel comfortable in your own skin you need to ensure that your daily actions and the overall direction of your life are congruent with who you say you are. Refer to your values constantly to ensure you're living up to your own standards. Keep your word. No one else may notice but *you will*. Keep it real.

5. *Take pride*.
Hold yourself with pride. You're terrific. You're making the effort to lead a good life, the best life possible. Enjoy the feeling. Smile. And when you fall short of your standards on the odd occasion, relax. It'll stop you getting pious! You're human too.

Be good!

6

Let it Go

I grew up a Catholic in Northern Ireland. I know all about guilt! I was educated by nuns at a convent from the ages of four to eighteen. I'm very familiar with the notion of us human beings being intrinsically stained with that original sin, flawed from birth. Thankfully, there was always the confessional box, which I made full use of! Every Saturday morning I'd take myself off to St Peter's Church in downtown Lurgan and have my sins washed away, and it was quite wonderful.

I'd arrive laden down with the weight of my badness, my poor soul stained and muddied as a result. Five minutes declaring those sins to a sympathetic priest in complete confidence, heartfelt atonement on my part, penance from him, absolution from God himself and I was on my way. Lighter and cleaner, I'd skip back home up North Street with my beautiful soul once more whiter than white! Happiness!

I want that same lightness for you. The difference is that you have to do the penance and absolution all by yourself; unless of course you're already a fan of the confession box, in which case you may already be fine! Otherwise you're going to have to follow my altogether more secular approach.

Somehow, you have to figure out a way of understanding yourself and God that doesn't leave you indelibly wrong, guilty, a sinner. A working, more liberating perspective is one that sees God in everything and everyone and that includes you.

See yourself as part of a divine organizing intelligence, a loving God force, which is the creative spirit behind everything, which is eternal, universal and never dies.

The label isn't important but your relationship with it is. Seeing yourself as part of this force, that you have a divinity within you, encourages you to honour yourself, to treat yourself with kindness, compassion and dignity.

In my earlier book, *Be Your Own Life Coach*, I suggested creating a small altar in your bedroom to appreciate yourself and this sacred perspective. At the very least, find a photograph of yourself when you were about four, looking absolutely adorable. Frame that picture and place it where you see it every day. Look at your younger self with loving compassion. You're the picture of innocence. Why would you ever see yourself as anything other than precious, worthy and valuable, then, now and for ever? Why would you ever think of yourself as anything other than entirely deserving of love, happiness, everything great that life could offer? You're divine, a living, breathing, pulsing particle of God.

Sometimes I've come across people who treat themselves as if they're so inherently bad that life is one big, long, slow punishment. They're generous to a fault, the fault being that they exclude themselves from their generosity. They cheer on and delight in their friends' success and progress but can't, won't, do the same for themselves. How skewed is that? Except it makes total sense if you feel yourself to be intrinsically bad at your core, different from others, undeserving.

The most pressing, the most urgent issue you'll face in your secular world is that of forgiveness. Without the confessional box, or something similar, you're on your own. You absolutely *must* get comfortable with the concept of forgiveness in your life. You need to become adept at spotting when blame and guilt are taking a hold, and deal swiftly and decisively with the issue. Right now it's highly likely that you are harbouring grudges against yourself. It would be unusual if you did not blame or resent yourself for pain that you feel you were responsible for. Continually wounding yourself with recrimination and regret just won't do. Picking and scratching at yourself keeps the wound from closing and healing. Open and oozing, it trickles venom, slowly poisoning and undermining you, warping the way you feel about yourself. You may already have thought deeply about all of this and wiped the slate clean for yourself, but, in my experience, it is rare. You're more likely to have kept yourself on a hook, suspended from full forgiveness and release. Soon, I'm going to throw you a challenge: to liberate and forgive yourself for everything you hold against yourself, to let go of the past and stride out.

My work as a coach requires me to identify obstacles in the path of my client's progress through life. Occasionally, a person will struggle to feel enthusiastic about their future because they don't feel deserving of happiness. One such client, Louise, had been working on call through the night as a junior doctor. She was called to an emergency caesarean which went horribly wrong and resulted in the death of the baby. Had Louise acted differently the outcome might have not been fatal. Although she was cleared of responsibility for the baby's death by the formal inquiry, Louise blamed herself and her life became one long, grim punishment. She came to me overwhelmed with guilt, feeling she deserved nothing better than her present misery. Gradually Louise began to forgive herself, seeing the circumstances of that awful event in a truer perspective. Interestingly, she saw God as all merciful and admitted that He would certainly forgive her. This was her turning point as she slowly became accustomed to the notion of forgiving herself.

We also identified the covert ways in which she punished herself: never having any time for herself, at the beck and call of her husband and small son; never going out socially; never doing anything for herself, only for others. She had turned her life into sheer drudgery. Over a period of months Louise felt able to lift her head and feel deserving of happiness. The art of forgiveness was probably her biggest life lesson.

His Holiness the Dalai Lama says: 'Forgiveness means that you no longer harbour anger or hatred towards an individual, or a group. What use is it to keep ill feeling towards others? It doesn't help to solve the problem; it just destroys your peace of mind, and usually your health, too. The alternative is a form of self-torture.'

Archbishop Desmond Tutu, who chaired South Africa's controversial Truth and Reconciliation Commission, has thought deeply about this notion of forgiveness too. He says: 'Forgiving is not easy. Forgiving means abandoning your right to pay back the perpetrator in his own coin but, in my experience, it is a loss which liberates the victim. Forgiving is not being sentimental.'

One of the reasons I left Northern Ireland as soon as I could was that there seemed so little hope for forgiveness between the two warring communities. In stark contrast an entire nation recognized the importance of forgiveness in order to build a viable new future in South Africa.

Don't be at war with yourself. Please show the same kindness, compassion, understanding and forgiveness to yourself as you would to another person. Be reconciled to yourself. Draw a line under the past and move on. Guilt, blame and resentment will putrefy and poison your system. Left to fester, they'll demand punishment. They'll create conflict, confusion and war within you, about you. Happiness, contentment, joy and vibrant health find it hard to flourish in this environment. To forgive means to 'give for', to 'replace' the ill feeling, to gain a sense of harmony again. To forgive literally means to 'give up' that which you have been holding onto. Hate and self-loathing of any kind scar your picture of yourself, preventing you from seeing yourself as worthwhile as others.

Hopefully, you'll never have to face up to your own forgiveness in anything like Louise's extreme example. But we humans seem to have an inbuilt propensity for self-blame and guilt. As children we notoriously blame ourselves for just about any routine misfortune, whether it's our parents' divorce, their financial difficulties, our failure to pass that exam, their long hours at work, anything. Yesterday my twelve-year-old son, Jamie, treated next door's dog to a huge ice-cream, which she thoroughly enjoyed. Five minutes later, she heaved the entire thing up again on the pavement. Jamie blamed himself and felt guilty for the rest of the day and all he'd done was spend his pocket money treating the dog.

Unless you've had *really* smart parents, then you'll have acquired your own bespoke list of 'reasons to feel bad about myself'. Take a good look at your life. Are you punishing yourself? Are you feeling unworthy because of things that have happened or people that you've hurt? Are you suspending feeling worthy and deserving until you've lost weight, given up smoking, made some change? If you believe you've done something wrong or that there's something inherently wrong with you, you'll feel you don't deserve great things from life. You'll suppress your desires and inhibit their fulfilment. You have to know that you're as worthy to receive whatever it is you want as any other person on the planet. Feeling worthy is the essence of being at peace. You have to be at peace.

LET IT GO

1. *Tell the truth.*

Write this down, 'What I blame myself for'; 'What I resent myself for'; 'What I don't forgive myself for'. Begin these lists now and keep them open for a full day, adding to them as more items occur to you. Some of these grudges will be easy to dismiss and laugh at, others more complex. Refine your lists so that you end up with a final shortlist. At this stage, just get them down on paper so that you we know what you're dealing with.

2. *Show compassion.*

Ask yourself this crucial question: 'What do I *really* need to forgive myself for?' What are you really blaming yourself for? Take the most serious charge you have levelled at yourself. Look at the situation as though it had happened to a close, dear friend. What would you say to them to encourage them to see the wider picture – all the mitigating circumstances? Make a case, a really good one, for them to show compassion, to cut themselves some slack. This is absolutely not the same as making excuses for oneself or shirking responsibility for one's actions. On the contrary, this is actually fronting up, acknowledging what's happened, making amends and moving on. By simply living with the bad memory, torturing and depriving yourself, you are indulging your guilt to no good purpose whatsoever. Get over it. Face your guilt head-on; take the decision right now to begin to forgive yourself. All you need to set this in motion is a *willingness*. Write down now, 'I am now willing to forgive myself for . . .'

3. *Do penance not punishment.*

To successfully move on without holding an underlying grudge against yourself, feeling genuinely contrite is imperative. You've got to be truly sorry. Obviously the more significant the event, the more relevant this becomes. I trust you to keep a perspective here. If there really is something that eats away at you, that prevents you from living fully, then you need to admit contrition and make amends. The pace at which you do this is entirely up to you. Don't skim over this heartfelt contrition but don't dwell too long on it either. People can spend their entire lives here and end up professional lifelong martyrs. That's pure indulgence. Let's move on.

4. *Make amends.*

It's one thing to feel genuine remorse for one's actions. It's quite another to show it. But show it you must. You must demonstrate your remorse for yourself in order to feel genuinely worthy of your absolution. How can you do this? The person or persons involved may no longer be with you; the event in question may be of no concern to anyone other than yourself. You must decide on your best course of action. Just do it immediately. Call it instant karma or payback time. Give generously of your time, money or expertise to someone or something. Don't make a speech about it. Don't draw any attention or admiration to yourself. *You* are the real beneficiary here. Keep it pure.

5. *Lighten up.*

At this point in your plan, relax! Lighten up. Smile. Breathe a little bit more deeply. You're doing all the right things. What more can you do? Probably nothing beyond reminding yourself that you're only human. You're on a quest for perfection. Keep enjoying the journey. Keep doing the best you can and well done, you for even trying. Learn the lesson from all your actions. There might not even be one, other than don't be so darned hard on yourself.

When I was thirteen I was both a swot and a daddy's girl. A combination that led me to cheat – very badly – in an exam.

Shame was heaped on me. My dad was called to take me off the school premises immediately. Another dad might have heaped on yet more shame. Luckily mine had a sense of humour and was a bigger person than any of the Sisters of Mercy nuns at my convent school. He could see I'd learned my lesson and merely pointed out that I was only trying to do as well as possible. Sometimes perspective is everything! Keep your cool. When you've done all you can and should, leave it. Wipe the slate clean.

Remember. You're valuable, totally worthy, utterly deserving. Come on. You're divine. Drop it.

Let it go.

7

Stand Out

In the 1950s the American State of Georgia was a place of black and white segregation. There were separate toilets, restaurants, schools, and even beaches for blacks and whites. Buses had chains to keep whites at the front and blacks at the back. In this atmosphere a young Irish priest lived and worked in one of the poorest areas of Savannah. Father Jim was the Principal of St Pius V, an all-black secondary school. It had an outstanding basketball team. They were unbeatable, winning the Negro Estate League championship in 1953. Father Jim applied for membership of the Catholic League, which would allow them to play a greater range of teams and really stand out. Membership was refused. It was only open to white teams.

Not easily foxed, Father Jim suggested a match between their finest, The Sacred Heart, and his team. This was agreed upon, on the condition that the St Pius team came alone, with no supporters. Fine. Father Jim's boys 'lost' the match by four points. A further match was arranged, as per custom, to take place at the losing side's school. Father Jim generously invited the Sacred Heart team to bring along their families and supporters in equal numbers to the St Pius team. The assembly hall was divided equally down the middle and an extraordinary event took shape. The St Pius team won effortlessly, beating their opponents by thirty points. The *real* point was that it showed up the bigotry and prejudice that prevented kids from even playing games together or being educated alongside each other in the same classroom. The real triumph was giving those black teenagers the opportunity to see how brilliant, how completely outstanding they were, against any team, black or white, and, that they were equal to anyone. If they could be the best there on the basketball court, then why not elsewhere in other areas of life? Who knows what difference that day made to them or to anyone else present? Who knows what part it played, along with many other acts of defiance, in the eventual repeal of segregation? It would be another ten years until the Civil Rights Act of Congress abolished all public segregation laws throughout the US.

In this, and many, many other acts of a similar nature, Father Jim was simply doing 'the right thing', the only thing he felt he could do in that situation. He never asked for personal reward, glory or fame. Universal Studios may never make a film of his life. The only reason you're reading about it now is that Father James Harrold is my uncle, my father's older brother. And the only reason I got to hear about it is that my brother Brian passed through Savannah recently on a business trip and visited the area where my uncle had lived and worked. Brian spoke with people who had been Father Jim's pupils and parishioners, who remembered our uncle clearly and spoke vividly of him, and you're hearing about it now, fifty years later. My brother says the area has not changed a great deal. As Father Jim says, 'You can change laws, but changing people's hearts takes a lot longer.' The world is far from perfect. There is still a huge need for people to stand out as Father Jim did – and continues to – back in Ireland, fit and fabulous at eighty-five.

Martin Luther King said that not everyone can be famous but everyone can be great. Doing the right thing, and knowing that nobody else knows about it, is real greatness. *You* can be great any time you like. The timing is down to you. The opportunities are everywhere. You choose.

You never really know who you are until you see yourself in action. You can *know* yourself to be generous, but unless you *do* something that displays generosity, you have nothing but a concept. You can *know* yourself to be kind, but unless you *do* someone a kindness, you have nothing but an *idea* about yourself. Until you see active service, you can only speculate about yourself. Turn your grandest concepts about yourself into your greatest experience, then, you will have the proof that shows who you are. Knowing is not enough. Your actions tell you who you really are, and who you can be.

In the chapter, 'Be Good', I spoke of the need for personal values. Now I'm suggesting that you consider the application of these values and attitudes. Look to see whether the values you serve, with your actions, bring about the highest and best expression of you. Examine your values one by one. Hold them up to the light of public scrutiny. If you can tell the world who you are and what you believe without hesitating or running, you are happy with yourself. You will have created a self – and a life – which needs no improvement. You will have reached perfection.

We live in dangerous times. We have great numbers of teenagers who appear to have no inherent sense of right and wrong, good or bad, and who lack moral guidelines or conscience to restrain their behaviour. They have no sense of family, of responsibility, or of community. The absence of positive male role models is dire. The failure of religion to offer moral leadership often means that children are raised in a total moral vacuum. Soaps and a playstation fill the gap. What's all this got to do with you, you might be thinking. Well, only you can decide that. But, make no mistake, each one of us is faced with a choice. Like it or not, your choice is to stand by and sigh or to stand up and do something. For evil to flourish, all it takes is for good people to do nothing, nothing at all. Standing by and sighing is a covert decision. It's a choice. It indicates a feeling of powerlessness and resignation. Good people like you need to be powerful. It's not about the power. It's about the influence. The world needs you to overcome your hesitation and be a force for good. Whatever you feel prompted to do, just do it. You don't need a Ph.D. in 'Making a Difference' to make a difference. Make your move. You already know how you could take a stand. Get on with it. We need more heroes. Push yourself forward. Speak out and champion your chosen cause. Never mind who's looking at you. Forget about looking good. Your cause is more important than your embarrassment.

Your contribution can be more low-key as well. It is obvious that children and teenagers are the ones in most urgent need of help. There is so much that someone like you can do as an individual; many organizations could put your goodwill to good use. Helping to teach a fourteen year old to read and write better could be the best thing anyone's ever done for him, and *you* could do it. Once enough good people stand up and resolve to make a difference, then change is unstoppable. Think Mahatma Gandhi, Martin Luther King, Nelson Mandela, the Pankhurst sisters, John F. Kennedy, Aung San Suu Kyi, the Burmese leader, and even recently, former New York Mayor, Rudi Guiliani. The Experience Corps was launched in Britain in February 2002. This is the biggest national volunteer programme to be launched by any government since World War II. Full-page ads in newspapers are calling for fifty year olds and over to enlist and make their 'wealth of experience' of use to young people. The carefully worded ad says: 'It won't come with a salary, but it will offer something of much greater value. Because whether you're a chief executive, an electrician or a lawyer, you'll find that nothing beats the satisfaction of being a caretaker too.'

Sometimes we have to feel driven to extremes before we feel called into action. Writing two days after 3,000 people lost their lives in the worst terrorist attack in living memory, the writer Philip Norman spoke of the profound changes the tragedy had brought about. Living in New York in the eighties, in the very shadow of the World Trade Center, he had come to think of it as a city without a heart. By 13 September all that had changed. He recalled the previous selfishness and self-absorption of New Yorkers, in particular their total indifference towards the suffering of others; how, for all the city's stupendous wealth, you would see beggars there more pitiable than in the worst cities of the Third World. However, from the moment disaster struck reports came of New Yorkers realizing they were not, as they had always thought, a divided uptown and downtown, but a community, facing a crisis such as none in America had known since the Civil War. Americans have always admired Britain's 'Blitz spirit', during World War II, but in Manhattan just such a spirit awoke. Hospitals devoted their energies to treating the seriously hurt, comforting and counselling the traumatized. No one even thought of asking to see a credit card. People opened their homes to the shell-shocked. Restaurants sent out relays of food to sustain the rescue workers. New York, Norman concluded, had become a richer place. It might have lost the greatest modern symbol of its wealth and power. But it had found its heart again. What happened on 11 September has made each of us question what is crucial to our lives. As office workers in suits dived from windows, airline passengers attacked hijackers with butter knives, and stock markets signalled a global depression, most of us began to re-evaluate the point of life. Hopefully it will make us realize that it's not all about a bigger house, a better car, a new conservatory, shares and pensions. Now all that matters is leading a decent life today.

STANDING OUT

1. *Be powerful.*
Good people like you need to push forward and fill positions of power and influence in public life. Drop all coyness and take every opportunity to advance yourself. If not you, then who – perhaps someone less scrupulous. You owe it to yourself and all of us to have a go. Do something today to make you feel proud.

2. *Live an important life.*
Make your life important by making it above average, beyond the making and spending of money. There *has* to be more to life than this. Ensure that yours is. Involve yourself in a cause close to your heart or conscience. See the difference you can make. Think global and act local. Someone as smart as you has the wherewithal to prevent mobile phone masts being erected next to your local primary school or to round up neighbourhood resistance to the property developers threatening to 'redevelop' your local shops into luxury apartments. People just like you do all of this.

3. *Be different.*
Each day brings opportunities for big gestures. Say thank you with conviction and style. Appreciate others, put it in writing or with flowers. Living a grand life entails acting with grace and generosity. Big people never act small or mean. Big people drop everything to run to their best friend when she's collapsing under everything, even

when she say's she's fine. Even your choice of washing-up liquid can be the act of someone choosing to do their bit for a cleaner earth. Daily acts of kindness and generosity will make you big, will elevate you and your life. Light up someone's day with a smile or a kind word, and they'll do the same for you. You'll increasingly take on the demeanour of someone who's *different* from the norm, a cut above. And you are!

4. *Keep it light.*

Avoid getting weighed down with the enormity of all that you want to do. Don't get heavy. Do your bit and stay cheerful. It's a discipline. All spiritual masters maintain cheerfulness diligently, regardless of the suffering in their midst. Work at keeping your spirit lifted. If you're slipping into misery, pull back. Take a break and regain your perspective.

5. *Keep it pure.*

Resist calling attention to your good deeds. Don't broadcast it. Your reward is knowing that you're brilliant. Your greatness comes from seeing yourself stand out from the crowd. And, of course, life is never dull. You live a far more interesting life than those who stand still. You'll meet some great people. The rush of seeing yourself in active service, making a difference, keeps you interesting and young. Be big. Choose great. Choose outstanding. *You're* the real beneficiary.

Stand out.

8

Fake It

I first learned the importance of faking it when I was no more than twelve or thirteen. I was deeply impressed with the new female newsreaders on television, Angela Rippon and Anna Ford, and I decided that this might well be my future too. I discussed the idea with my darling, doting dad, who thought it splendid and offered his wholehearted support. We decided that a strong Belfast accent might not be quite the thing for the BBC evening news, regional variations on the Queen's English being a more recent trend. Immediately we set upon the task of refining my accent, softening and polishing my every word so that I could have come from anywhere. I went to school the next day sounding more Malone Road than the Mourneview estate of the previous day (Malone Road being Belfast's Eaton Square and the Mournview estate being something quite different altogether). I was faking it and loving it. And it worked, perfectly. Admittedly I'm not reading the news but then I changed my mind about that anyway. Don't get me wrong. I am not the least embarrassed about coming from 77 Russell Drive and I have no regrets about anything in my previous life. I just didn't love the accent that went with it. I knew it wouldn't travel well. After all, it's not where you've come from that's important – it's where you're going.

I have carried on faking it throughout my life and shall probably carry on for the rest of it. It's been an invaluable asset to me and taken me to all sorts of interesting places and social situations. That's not to say I'm a fake. Integrity, honesty and authenticity are hugely important to me. I'm very real. It's just that I loathe limitation. So if imitation and acting the part make one's passage through life easier and more fun, I'm all for it. Never mind finding out who you are. The question is, who do you want to be? Because the truth is, you could be anyone. Children know this instinctively. Unless, that is, they've been schooled to think otherwise. My twelve-year-old son Jamie made this announcement as I drove him to school the other day: 'Anyone could do anything, anything they wanted to do. They could learn to play the piano, the guitar, do anything, go anywhere, be anything they wanted to be. They just need to learn how to do it.' This was a real Eureka! moment for Jamie. He'll bank this and draw on it from time to time over the years. If I'm lucky, he'll base his entire life on this single insight.

Obviously, we in the developed world have far more freedom than our neighbours in other nations and it's worth remembering this occasionally. So, let me be absolutely clear with you what I'm really talking about here. Faking it, as I practise it, is the bridge between where you are right now and where you want to be. This gap has to be closed and the challenge for you is to close that gap as fast and imaginatively as you can. In other words, you can redesign, reinvent yourself any time, any place. Paul McKenna is one of the world's leading stage hypnotists and a multi-millionaire from sales of his shows, tapes and books. He has had his own television series and is to be found at the best parties and premières. At twenty-nine he was a little-known radio DJ. One day he interviewed a hypnotist on his show and was captivated. He determined there and then to train and forge an exciting new life for himself. He knew that to pull it off he would have to *appear* confident, relaxed, entirely self-assured. So he began to *act like this type of person*. So convincing is he that he's clearly become the person he always wanted to be – a triumph of self-invention.

Learning to act the part is vital. The better the act, the more real you are, and the more quickly the gap closes. How else do actors convincingly play the part of characters completely different from themselves? They identify the mannerisms and behaviour of their chosen role and then inhabit that persona. They wear it like a cloak so their previous self is concealed. When they do it thoroughly enough, we are convinced. If they do it long enough, *they* are convinced. This 'Method' school of acting often makes it extremely difficult for the actor to shake off the adopted persona.

For his role in the film, *The Boxer*, Daniel Day-Lewis trained full-time for *two years* before filming even began. He moved to Ireland to train with Irish boxing champion, Barry McGuigan, running six miles and sparring in the ring six days a week. Eventually, in McGuigan's opinion, he was good enough to go professional and the film went on to pick up three Golden Globes. This is faking it so well that it becomes real. You become the very thing you ape and desire to be. The mistake many people make is in giving up before they make it real. They feel ill at ease. They feel they're faking it. Of course they are. It's the easiest, and sometimes the only, way to make it to the other side. *Act as if* is a big recovery term in AA. Act as if you believe you will stay sober. Act as if you like meetings. Act as if you believe in God. Act as if you like praying. Act as if you believe in the Twelve Steps. And, soon enough, so it shall be.

Faking it is the title of one of the UK's most popular television series. Each programme features one brave person ready to take up the challenge to completely transform their identities. One of the most impressive was Ed, a burger-van vendor who had to 'fake it' as a top haute-cuisine London chef in just four weeks. Ed's challenge was to convince a panel of expert judges that he was a genuine head chef. Learning the trade in the kitchen of notorious chef Gordon Ramsay, Ed needed to master not only the necessary culinary skills, but also the swagger and bluster of a temperamental top chef. One of Ed's most serious problems was exerting authority and an acting coach was given the job of turning Ed into a fierce, arrogant chef. This was no mean challenge for someone who hated telling people what to do. 'I'd rather curl up and die,' said Ed. Ed's biggest problem was simply being too nice to do the job properly.

Gradually we saw him getting into the part, deepening and projecting his voice to issue instructions, goading and cajoling his team to get a move on, exerting authority and leadership. Finally judgement day arrived. Ed and his team competed against three groups of professional chefs from some of London's finest kitchens. Could he convince the judges that he was a pro – or would they know he was just faking it? Ed was masterful and magnificent. Focused, determined, driven, he barked orders at his team, pulling them together to deliver a superb meal on time. In the sweltering heat of the kitchen, under the gaze of judges and cameras, he kept it together. He looked the part and carried it off to convince the judges that he was for real. Not only that but he actually won the competition against professionals with years of experience. A class act.

I believe that great achievers everywhere understand the importance of faking it. Anna Wintour, British editor-in-chief of American *Vogue*, is a case in point. Hugely successful in the cut-throat world of US publishing, she is known as Nuclear-Wintour for her glacial manner. Personally I think she's fabulous and a darned fine model for busy women, especially if getting out of the office at a decent hour to see your kids is important. Her decisiveness is legendary. In a recent documentary she admitted to 'acting decisive', even when she doesn't feel it. When offered the choice of a black or white skirt for the cover shot, she'll not hesitate to bark an unequivocal answer. Without delay or doubt a decision is reached. Explaining, she simply points out that her position requires her to be seen as decisive. Her staff need her to act this way. She has a lot to get through and, at the end of the day, it's only fashion. Regardless of how she feels, she acts decisive. I don't doubt that many of her decisions are genuinely felt. Others will be polished faking. A pure professional.

Even the great wartime hero Churchill understood the importance of looking and acting the part. He conveyed strength and confidence at all times to inspire faith in his leadership and uphold the fighting spirit of the British people. Regardless of setbacks, he consistently convinced the nation that victory was imminent and inevitable. Regardless of how he felt inside, he acted strong and confident on the outside. This was entirely appropriate to the role and responsibility he held. More recently, ex-New York mayor Rudi Guiliani has been praised for his presidential demeanour in the wake of the 11 September attack in that city. Regardless of his personal turmoil and grief, his public face was strong and confident. Mindful of his need to show leadership and keep his people strong, he was labelled the 'real' President. Mr Guiliani said afterwards that he had been following the example of Churchill in appearing strong and confident. His duty required nothing less.

FAKING IT FOR REAL

1. *You could be anyone.*

   Who do you want to be? Decide how you want to be seen. What sort of person do you want to come over as? What are the primary characteristics, personality traits? Cheerful, easygoing, generous? Supremely confident, self-assured and self-possessed? All of this and more? Decide. Work at it. The more you work at it, the more convincing you'll be to others – and yourself. Remind yourself on the hour of who you are. Soon you won't need to. It will be real.

2. *Make it real.*

   You can't practice your new persona alone. You need to 'out' yourself in public. You need practice and you need people to practise on. Take every opportunity to perform in front of others. Take tea at Claridges, champagne at the Savoy. Put on your chosen demeanour, act the part. Exude confidence, ease and bonhomie. Don't feel your fear, ignore it. Just strike the pose. Your mind will catch up with your body and you'll soon feel as good as you look.

3. *Dress to conquer.*

   Appearances are important. Ask anyone who's gone from brunette to blonde, from size twenty to size ten. Looking the part is half the battle. Actors often say that they only really get into the part when they dress for the part. What is your dress code? How do you need to look? If dropping ten pounds brings you closer to the real you, get on with it. Those who can afford it employ 'stylists' to present the right image. Think Madonna, Kylie, Tina Turner and every pop band in the world. Stylists and their image control are so prized and sought after nowadays they are turning into stars in their own right, Right now, Katie Grand in the UK, responsible for Madonna's latest cutting-edge look, is fêted and interviewed in her own right.

4. *Does the name fit?*
Are you comfortable being Doris, Mervyn, Ruby or Dean? Or if you're a show-business baby, Fifi Trixibelle or Honey Delight? There is absolutely no reason why you should stick with the name that you've been given. Change it. Go from Tracy to Frankie, Pratt to Jones, whatever. I happen to love the name Fiona but if I was called by my confirmation name, Martina, it just wouldn't work. I'm a Fiona, never a Martina. Is it any wonder Elton John dropped the name Reg Dwight or Sting stopped being Gordon Sumner or Marie McLaughlin became Lulu? Denise van Outen sounds much more interesting than plain old Denise Outen. And Norma Jeane Baker just *had* to become Marilyn Monroe. My great friend, the novelist Lennox Morrison, used to be Margaret. But she was never *really* a Margaret, always a Lennox in waiting. Along with the name, Lennox changed her shape and career, securing one of those two-book deals you read about. So, there's a lot in a name. If yours doesn't fit, get a better one. Be true to who you are now.

5. *Move on.*
If you're a gay teenager in Nebraska or North Shields you'll need to head for New York or London or similar to be around people like you. New York in particular is a place where people go to find out who they are and be whoever they want. Everyone can find their group there, whether it's cultural, ethnic or a lifestyle group. You need to live somewhere where you can feel most alive, where you can make a home and feel able to express yourself. London is big enough to let you start over; to make a new beginning just by moving from Brixton to Hampstead, Barnes to Islington.

Remember, it's not where you've come from that counts, it's where you're going. Have fun along the way. When you need to,

Fake it.

9

Get Lucky

I've been a people-watcher for as long as I can remember, for ever really. I used to adore hanging out in hotels and restaurants with my dad just to watch. The food was never the thing; often we just took tea if it was a really swanky place. We were there for the people. From Portadown to Palma, we watched. So I couldn't believe my luck when, at fourteen, I got the job of coat girl on Saturday nights at the smartest hotel around, the Seagoe Hotel. Here, I could watch people close-up *and* get paid for it. Heaven. Philomena Begley and her Ramblin Men did their thing on stage while I did mine in the cloakroom. I was invisible to all the dancing girls and dining couples but I was free to learn. I've seen a lot since then. But I've never got jaded. I'm as fresh and alert as I was twenty-five years ago about this whole business of life and the best way to go through it. What I want more than anything, I guess, is to feel that I'm living the best, most interesting life possible, for me, that I'm not missing out on something better, someplace else. I'm not sure if it's the same for everyone, but isn't it the same for you? Why else read this book – there are loads of other books you could be reading. It's no coincidence that it's this one. Therefore, I'm going to presume that you're as eager as I am to lead a really great life.

So, I want you to make your life as easy and terrific for yourself as possible. I want to pass on what could be most useful to you. In all my years of observation, both paid and unpaid, what I've seen is this. I've seen that there's a certain type of person who leads a much, much easier life than others. These people we call 'lucky'. We say they lead a 'charmed life', they appear 'blessed'. Or is it 'good karma'? They have the luck of the devil, the luck of the Irish. No matter where they fell or into what, they'd still look good and smell fabulous. Doors open, invitations and opportunities come in droves, good fortune is their natural state. More often, they're in the right place at the right time. They're just one big serendipity force field. And – dammit – they're so darned cool! What do they know that others don't? What's their secret?

I'm not sure they could tell you. But I think I can. They're my favourite people. I adore them. I look out for them and hang out with them as much as possible. They're my kind of people. I can spot them on sight. I met a taxi driver the other day and knew *instantly* that he was one. I spent the first twenty-one years of my life in close proximity to one – my dad – and I saw him operate. And then I looked around and noticed that my older brother Brian was one as well! That's lucky. I came across a story recently about one man's life and death that I found absolutely riveting. This is it.

On 20 February 2001, Mark Simpson literally stopped the traffic in central London. His funeral took place at Holy Trinity Church in Sloane Avenue. Cars were backed up to Piccadilly while an assistant Bishop of London led his cortège around Sloane Square, its pavements lined with high-profile mourners from Manhattan and London. Yet his beginnings were far from grand. Just who was Mark Simpson? Mark was only forty-three when he died from meningitis. His love affair with the upper echelons had begun thirty-five years earlier, when he watched, on television, Churchill's coffin being paraded down

Whitehall and wondered aloud how he too might have such a send-off.

Mark grew up as the adopted son of a vicar. He was determined to work with the royal family. At just seventeen, having been previously turned away for being too young, he was finally offered a job in the royal nursery and the next decade was his dream come true. Mark accompanied the Prince of Wales to Australia and the Queen to Saudi Arabia; he sailed on the royal yacht, *Britannia*, and stayed at Sandringham and Balmoral. Then, somehow, the royal servant managed to slip through the social net. Somehow, the kind of people on whom he had waited came to want him as their house guest and confidant. Mark always felt himself to be more upstairs than downstairs. The great and the good all spoke of him as 'thoughtful, kind, generous, funny, charming, incredibly endearing and trustworthy'. He made powerful friends, moved to Manhattan, where he imported British antiques, and spent weekends at his boyfriend's house in the Hamptons. In the mid-nineties, he teamed up with Lucy Fox (now Countess Gormanston) to create Fox & Simpson, showing rich Americans around the stately homes of Britain. 'The thing about Mark,' said the socialite, Ivana Miller, 'was that he went through life on cloud nine, always believing things would turn out all right.' And they probably would have done. Even towards the end of his life when his business folded – apparently he was hopeless with money – and he had to stay with friends, albeit in Chelsea, Mark remained irrepressible. Just before he died he was introduced to the manager of the singer, Robbie Williams, who told him that Robbie needed a personal assistant. Mark interviewed for the job, which came with a flat, and he seemed assured of landing it. The society magazine *Tatler* put it this way: 'Mark was someone who made his life out of nothing, lived it like a long weekend, and left it halfway through.'

There are two things that really strike me about Mark. He clearly rose through life with the sheer force of his mesmeric personality. People, possibilities, great opportunities all came to him, in great measure. Some will have looked at him with awe and envy, failing to understand his immense appeal. But it's abundantly clear to me why he was so very attractive. He was simply a joy to know and be around. I also admired his grit. He was no mere dandy. He pushed for what he wanted: a glamorous life in the company of the royal family. He made it happen. Initially rejected for being too young he persisted and when his chance did come his knowledge of the history and tradition of the royal family was so impressive that he was given the job on the spot. He made good use of his contacts and opportunities to forge his own role in life, on both sides of the Atlantic. Mark made his luck. He could probably have taught us all a thing or two.

Let's be clear. These people *do* exist. It's not folklore. And it's all true. They really are lucky. They're special. The sum total of the parts of their personality make for one powerful package. You definitely know at least one of these people. You may even be one yourself. They 'got lucky' when character was being handed down. They've got a lot going for them and it's all's natural. I'm talking charisma, warmth, charm, social ease, quick wit, generous spirit, natural optimism. It's all effortlessly there and they don't even know how lucky they are! Of course they get their fair share of setbacks and let-downs, but they're defiantly buoyant. They recover more quickly than most. They've got more bounce. And they're never, ever bitter. They just don't 'do' grudges. You can see why they're so attractive.

Don't you want some of this for yourself? Of course you do. There is absolutely no reason why you can't opt for more good fortune, ease, flow and downright luck. These naturally lucky people all share a number of patterns, characteristics and habits. There is absolutely no reason why you can't share them too. I believe I have accurately identified the five key factors that these individuals all have in common. I am convinced that I have come up with a winning formula. I know it works because I've used it with clients to great effect and, obviously, I wouldn't want you experimenting with something that I hadn't thoroughly tested on myself first. You can learn these habits, adapt them for yourself and get the same results. Yes, I know that some people get to be born into great houses with doting parents. Never mind that. You can change your luck. Make your own luck. Your destiny is in your hands. You have free will. Anyway, money doesn't buy luckiness, though lucky people rarely go short. I'm going to take you through this winning formula. I will '*unconceal*' for you what makes these people so special. And they are. It's not magic. It's not complicated. But it is brilliant. And the more people there are around like this the better. Feelin' lucky? Come on . . .

GET LUCKY

1. *They ooze charm.*

I mean ooze. They're juicy. It pours out of them. They have impeccable manners and they work at it. They do please and thank you with style and sincerity. They give such genuine gratitude that they generate a flow of more of the same right back to themselves, although this is never their motive – it just happens that way. My great friend Simon does this masterfully. An actor, he reinvented himself at thirty-five into a travel journalist. Within three months he was earning more than twice his previous income, and securing commissions with the quality press and upmarket glossies. I have absolutely no doubt that his first-rate manners have been instrumental in bringing such good fortune his way. It marks him out and endears him to people. They remember him. On a recent press trip to the US he was upgraded to a business-class seat. On his return home, he called the press officer at British Airways to thank her. She was stunned. This was the first time in nearly twenty years that any journalist had bothered to call and say thank you. Simon makes a point of treating everyone with this same respect. He never takes people's kindness and generosity for granted. He has a lot to be thankful for, but that's down to him. Manners count. Finesse costs nothing.

2. *They work hard.*

Remember the saying, 'The harder I work, the luckier I get'? It's true. Lucky people don't leave their lives to fate. They are ingenious in getting their way. They try harder and longer than the average person. Sometimes they do it with sheer barefaced cheek as well; needs must. I had the good fortune to have lunch recently with one of the UK's leading and most respected journalists. I'll call her Jane. Everyone thinks of her life as being so easy and, you guessed it, lucky. I was eager to find out more. At nineteen she was studying interior design and architecture, and hating it. At school she had won prizes for her writing and she'd loved it. In the late 1970s D.C. Thompson, one of the UK's leading publishers, had offices in her home town of Dundee. Unannounced, she walked in one day, told them she could write and that she was looking for a job. She was taken up to the features department, given pen and paper and invited to write something. She wrote about her last kooky summer job on the Shetland Islands, handed it over and was offered a job on the spot. It gets better. Jane's passion at the time was music, especially the new punk bands that were just emerging in Britain in the late 1970s. She was given the position of pop editor on one of their national titles. Within a few days she was in Edinburgh, on tour with Bob Geldof and the Boomtown Rats. How cool is that?

3. *They take risks.*

They definitely live life with a certain aplomb. They thrive on the rush of the new, embracing change and adventure. When my brother Brian decided to leave Australia and return home to Ireland, he walked away from a glittering career, a secure future, a fabulous lifestyle and great friends to return to an Ireland with a very depressed economy. He had no job to step into, and only modest savings. He was also married with six young children. But he just knew it was time to make the move. He refused to take everyone else's advice to hang onto his house in Sydney, just in case. He was determined to burn all his bridges so there was no easy way back. They would just *have* to make it work. And, of course he did. But not without some scary times. Nevertheless, he pulled it off. You can read more of what happened to Brian in my first book, *Be Your Own Life Coach*. Suffice to say he's on the lookout for another change, and it's a really big one this time.

4. *They're great company.*

They make the effort. They extend themselves to include your interests in their conversation. And they are genuinely interested in you. They make every effort to make you feel at ease and welcome in their company. They do small talk really well, but then they've probably given it a lot of thought and practised hard. One of my clients, whose work involves travel, reads the local papers on the net to know what's topical in the part of the world he is visiting, whether it's the success of their local rugby team or a scandal involving a local politician, be it Savannah or Singapore. They also always look as though they're delighted to see you, and we all like to be liked. All of which makes it so easy to like *them*.

5. *They're generous.*

They give of themselves. They're generous with money, time, information, goodwill. They're big in spirit. They can afford to give of themselves because they instinctively feel all will be well in their world. And it usually is. Because whatever you give out comes back to you, multiplied. Therefore their natural optimism is constantly justified. They receive back in great abundance the very qualities that they embody and give out. They make the world a better place as a result, and live a pretty cool life in the process. They're 'happening' people and they're always going places.

Make the effort to be the same. Work at it.

Get lucky.

10

Great Expectations

Do you believe in fate? Is your future already mapped out? How much control do you really have over your life? Is your destiny preordained by forces beyond you? Does your karma go before you? In other words, how much of your life is in your hands? The answer is – you decide. It really is your choice. Your present life is shaped by the decisions you made in the past. Your future and your destiny will be the result of decisions you're making right now. The quality of those decisions is vital to your happiness, health, prosperity and fulfilment. There's a lot at stake here. My interest in influencing your decisions is to ensure that you get the best possible life – and the chance to reach your greatest potential.

My problem with relying on outside forces to provide you with an interesting life is that they're, well, outside you, beyond your control and influence. You have to wait and hope, and pray, and keep your fingers crossed. Don't get me wrong. I'm a big believer in the power of prayer, and faith, and God (more of that another time). I'm just uncomfortable with expecting someone else to do all the work. Crucially, taking responsibility for getting the life you want means that you crack on: you wait for nothing and no one. You figure out the best way forward, changing direction as you see fit, thinking fast, moving on. The very act of moving in the direction of your dreams and desires instantly makes life more interesting.

Let's be clear. Whatever your take on life, God and the universe, make it powerful. Ensure you're not abdicating responsibility to a higher power. Guidance is one thing. Leaving it all to fate or Divine Providence is something else. I appreciate that, sometimes, it's a fine line. My preference is to take total responsibility for making it all work, asking for and giving thanks for any help, seen and unseen, that comes my way in the process. So, watch your interpretation. If it renders you at the mercy of outside forces, think again.

Your life is your art, your own creation constantly in the making. You are designing it moment by moment with your every thought and the actions that follow. The really strange thing about us humans is our need to be right. It's definitely a design fault. Whatever we decide to be right about, we go out of our way to prove it, to prove we're right. I reckon the smartest thing to do is choose what you want to be right about. Then, automatically, you're on course to prove it. We adopt positions, take up opinions, then we stick to them, guard them, even fight to the death for them. Choose what you want to be right about. Make sure your position works well for you, gets you the result that you want. So, if you're looking for a great boyfriend or husband and your overriding expectation about men is that all the good ones are married and the rest are hopeless or gay, you're in trouble. You'll trip over Mr Fabulous sitting there, on his own, in your neighbourhood coffee shop. He doesn't exist – in your field of expectations and possibilities. Your radar is just not tuned into the frequency of great guys. So, to get the very thing, man, or woman, that you want, you have to be open to the possibility, the expectation, that, he, she, it actually exists. I used to do a column for the *Daily Mail*, called 'Dating Makeover', where I'd examine a reader's relationship history, pinpoint self-defeating patterns and set her on the right path to meet Mr Right. Nine times out of ten, these lovely women had given up, resigned to their fate. They actually no longer believed that a great guy was out there. Their expectations of meeting him and living happily for sometime to come were zilch. I'd confront them with this attitude and ask them, why bother even looking, when they were so sure what they were looking for didn't exist? I'd remind them that we were only looking for one great guy, not a whole army of them, just the one, in this vast city. Gradually, they would open up and raise their expectations to allow for the possibility. Otherwise, why bother? Another night out, another excuse to be right and resigned, again.

Assume with me, for a moment, that life is one great big self-fulfilling prophecy: that there are no surprises. In other words, we all get the life we *expect to get*. This would mean that we are our own soothsayers, that we have the ability to foresee our own future. How great would that be? I believe it's true. I believe that we get, very largely, what we expect to get. This might feel slightly scary because what it means is that your life, your entire future, is much more down to you than you may have previously admitted. It's also incredibly exciting. If we get what we expect, then expecting more, expecting the best, is vital. If our expectations influence our outcomes, then we had better make darned sure they're great expectations.

When I was about ten, I realized that I never expected to live in Northern Ireland. I realized that I expected to live in London. I saw my future stretching ahead of me, and it wasn't in Belfast. Some might say this was a premonition. I would say it was an exciting expectation, so compelling that it shaped the next decade of my life. I was happy to trade discos and dating for books and good grades so I could live the life I expected to, beyond Belfast. For me, university was my passport to the rest of the world. I never doubted, for a second, that I would fulfil my expectation. But I did work purposefully towards it for ten years. It was far too vital to leave to chance, fate, or God.

Respect your expectations. Rather, understand that whatever they are, however vague or covert, they're shaping your every move. Your decisions and actions, your entire life, are governed by unseen forces. They're not outside of you, *they're inside you.*

I've spoken to many people about their childhood expectations. The correlation between what they expected to get and what they got is staggering. One of the things I notice is that there was usually a significant adult who both fed and validated their expectations, however outrageous they appeared to be at the time.

Percy 'Master P' Miller is the world's richest rap star. His empire spans music, film, fashion and property. The 31-year-old rapper, real-estate broker, telecommunications provider, producer, actor, sports agent and general mogul-about-town has amassed a fortune estimated at $250 million (£175 million). Fortune magazine last year placed him twentieth on its list of the 'Forty Richest under Forty', two above fellow rapper Sean 'Puff Daddy/P Diddy' Combs, and way above Tiger Woods ($160 million).

When he was five Miller had, while sitting in a classroom, what he describes as a premonition. He saw himself as a wealthy, successful adult. Miller's grim New Orleans neighbourhood is riddled with violence and drug dealing. His younger brother Kevin was shot dead while still in his teens. In spite of his violent surroundings, Miller was a hardworking student. At eighteen he won a sports scholarship to the University of Houston and studied business communications. In 1990, armed with a cheque for $10,000 – the result of an insurance settlement following his grandfather's death, he opened a shop that sold rap records, videos and urban clothes. He called it No Limit – a catchphrase he adopted from the example set by his mother.

'My mom was an inspiration,' he says, 'a woman who raised five kids and took care of us, giving us the best she had. She taught me there don't have to be any limits.' Miller uses his early life to feed his motivation. 'If you don't want to live like that again you've got to work hard or you'll go back that way.'

The Pride of Britain Awards takes place each year to salute individuals for outstanding acts of courage and contribution. In 2002 Sandra Walton was named Teacher of the Year for transforming a failing school and the lives of the many children. In 1997 Pineapple Junior Infants School was a byword for failure. Its pupils were underachieving, attendance was low and morale among staff was plummeting. The year before, Standard Attainment Test (SATs) results showed it was the third-worst performing school in the country. Today, all that has changed thanks to the inspirational leadership of one woman. This year the government declared it one of the 100 most improved schools in the country. Sandra, fifty-six, was well aware of the extent of the task she was taking on. But after speaking to pupils and the community, she realized the school's enormous potential. She says: 'The first goal was to give the children high expectations of what they themselves could achieve – that there were no holds barred.'

Last year, all the hard work began to pay off with the publication of the school's SATs results. When Sandra took over, the mark was 72 out of 300 – last year it had risen to 216. Sandra Walton single-handedly taught those children to believe in themselves, to expect great things for and from themselves.

She held out high expectations for them. They followed her lead and their achievements reflect that. They stand a much better chance of a fulfilling life, with choices and opportunities as a result.

You can do the same for yourself. You can raise your expectations for yourself, by yourself, any time you like. It's never too late to think big. We all know, or know of, people who have achieved exactly what they wanted from life without the advantage of having an inspiring adult around when they were kids. It's just a lot easier that way. Thinking big is a habit, an acquired one. Even if you already have this habit, stay with me. You can always get better. If, like so many others, you don't like to 'raise your hopes', 'expect too much' so you 'won't get disappointed' or you like to be 'realistic', don't move.

GREAT EXPECTATIONS

1. *Expect more.*

We all know that raising children's aspirations and expectations is vital to their future success and achievements. So it is with you. Right now, write this down: 'Great expectations that I'm now holding for myself and my life'. Put something on this list immediately. Keep it open and add to it during the course of today. This is a fabulous and quick way to open your mind to exciting possibilities. You'll feel instantly energized by the prospect of great things coming your way. Get this: even if you were to do absolutely nothing practical about fulfilling these expectations, the very act of writing them down sets you on a course to receive them. Geri Halliwell recently found a wish list that she'd written many years previously, a long way before Ginger Spice and fame. All she had done was make a note of her desires. One of these was to have George Michael as a boyfriend – obviously this was before George had come out as gay. By the time she discovered her list, George was her closest friend. Your list is about what you'd really, really like. It's not for silly things like going from five foot two to five foot ten overnight. It's for things that, lift your spirit, even if you're only thinking about them, like driving along the pacific coast Highway from LA to Big Sur on a glorious sunny day, with Angie Stone on the stereo. Go on, what would do it for you?

2. *Expect the best.*

If your expectations really influence your outcomes, then you had better pay attention. Getting into the routine of anticipating the best outcome has to be carried out daily. Brush your teeth and don your habit. Focus on what you want, not on what you don't want. Anticipate success, the positive outcome of all that you're working on that day. Expect the best, every day, one day at a time.

3. *Trade up.*

Expectations can be outgrown. They need upgrading every so often. Expectations aren't for ever, they have a shelf-life. Check the sell-by date of yours to keep them fresh and vibrant. If you've outgrown earlier expectations, and life feels small or 'samey', you need to trade up. Firstly, look around at where you've taken yourself. Pat yourself on the back for your progress, right now. You've 'done good'. So, what fresh expectations would you like to buy into? Put them out there. Write them down. If they're great enough, you'll instantly feel relaxed and energized. You can see the way forward. Make it a good one.

4. *Expect to be liked.*

Life is so much easier and pleasanter if you assume that people will like you. You'll relax, smile more, breathe more often, your shoulders will drop into place, you'll look fresher, friendlier. And, guess what? People will respond differently to you. You'll feel more liked. Please don't take my word for it. Try it. Right now, choose to *expect to be liked*. Wherever you are right now, and for the rest of the day, anticipate that everyone you meet, on a bus, in a restaurant, in a shop, will warm to you, find you attractive and like you. If you're really adventurous – and single – expect men or women to find you, you know, sexy, glamorous, gorgeous, handsome, whatever. It all makes life that bit more interesting – and it works.

5. *Overhaul your expectations.*
It's easier to move forward if you're not being held back by negative expectations. They do exist. They're also likely to be someone else's cast-offs, utter rubbish, of no use to anyone, certainly not you. Begin to identify them immediately. Begin a list: 'Expectations I have held that restrict me and my life'. Keep this line of enquiry open, adding to it as garbage rises to the surface. Better out than in your psyche, causing unforeseen limitation.

Keep a watchful eye on your expectations. Understand that they're driving you. Check where they're taking you. Be rigorous. Insist on the best. Make sure they're

Great expectations.

11

Keep it Real

In the 1980s I adored the relationships expert Sondra Ray. I would turn up anywhere she was appearing. I'd be in the front row at the Loving Relationships Training centre in London, at the Harmonic Convergence in Glastonbury, and I very nearly made it to Hawaii for her Rebirthing and Physical Immortality workshop. Her books, *I Deserve Love, Loving Relationships* and *How to be Chic, Fabulous and Live Forever* were my gospel. I loved everything about her and everything she taught. I loved the New York glitz, the twang, the killer heels, the earrings, the 'permatan', the glorious glamour and polish of this fabulous woman.

But what I loved most of all, and the real reason I followed her, was that she was the most freed-up woman I'd ever come across. She opened her mouth and spoke the truth, her truth. She did it with complete conviction, clarity and ease. Nagging insecurities didn't feature. Niggling doubts didn't beset her. She didn't worry about what her audience might be making of her. Just pure, undiluted Sondra Ray and her take on self-esteem, losing weight, getting a boyfriend/girlfriend, making money, forgiving your parents and everyone else, living for ever. Just being around this totally composed, totally self-assured, down-the-line woman was the real lesson for me. Her presence alone inspired me. I modelled myself on her demeanour from the moment I set eyes on her, before she'd said a word.

She had personal power and poise written all over her. She oozed ease and comfort, she was utterly self-possessed. She had guts. She *approved* of herself. She didn't need the audience or anyone else to agree with her, think well of her, admire her. She didn't canvass the room for support before she declared her position. She already had the approval, respect and support of the most important person in the room − *herself.*

I loved the way she was always the same Sondra Ray. In August 1987 thousands of us gathered in Glastonbury, spiritual capital of the UK for the Harmonic Convergence, an event we thought would usher in a New World order of co-operation and peace. Sondra shared a platform with New Age gurus, dusty academics and professional hippies. Did she adapt to fit in? Not one jot. Sondra was Sondra, full-on yuppie glamour. Impeccably groomed from her carefully coiffeured head to her shiny Salvatore Ferragamo shoes, she oozed pure style, she had real substance. I learned the importance of self-approval from Sondra, though she never directly taught it. I learned the value of speaking the truth, speaking out without flinching or fearing for the response. I learned not to care in the best possible way.

This is what I want for you. I want you to be freed-up in the same way that Sondra was. I want you to know that being true to yourself is the real truth, whatever that is. Forget about being popular. It comes when you're not looking for it. Give up searching for respect, admiration and approval. You're looking in the wrong place. It all comes when you no longer *need* it. You want to be admired? Admire yourself. You want respect? Respect yourself. Approval? Go right ahead! Do it! Approve of yourself. What are you waiting for? Waiting for permission to think for yourself could take for ever and then never come. Far better to generate your own feel-good factors. Far, far better to look good in your own eyes, for yourself, than spend a lifetime trying to impress others. And the funny thing is that as soon as you've really cracked this, you'll have truckloads of respect, approval and admiration coming your way. People will be queuing up to give it to you, just when you no longer need it. That's the irony. When you do really grow up, into a mature, developed person who thinks for themselves, you stand out. You have presence. You have an air about you. There's something indefinably, distinctively different about you. You look as if you know things that others don't. You look cultivated. And you are. You've cultivated insight and wisdom. You've got depth. You're no longer average.

Don't you want this? Don't you relish the prospect of such freedom? Of course you do. Look around and spot the public figures you most admire. I'll bet they're people like Sondra – people who speak the truth. When they speak, you just know it's for real, it's the truth and nothing but the truth. Right now in the UK there's a debate raging about truth, what's real and what's spin. Spin is what politicians think we want to hear. Spin is canvassing focus groups to gauge what policies will be popular. Yet the government's craving and obsession with being popular is making them unpopular. Fence-sitting impresses no one.

There's now a groundswell desire for public figures to speak the truth, without having assessed its popularity beforehand. It is surely no coincidence that one of the most popular series in both the US and UK at the moment is *The West Wing* – critics have called it 'probably the best series ever made'. The programme is set in the west wing of the White House where the central character, President Josiah Bartlet (Martin Sheen), leads the most powerful nation on earth. President Bartlet is the real reason we watch. He exudes a charisma that belies his brilliance, his deep conviction and his dedication to what he believes is right for the country, despite the demands of numerous special interest groups. He regularly ignores the advice of his press secretary or delivers a completely different speech from the one that's been prepared earlier. Yet his staff are completely devoted to him because they see him as 'the real thing'. His primary conviction is to do the right thing and say what has to be said, regardless of how it affects his re-election campaign. How tragic is it that Martin Sheen plays a politician we admire purely because he's honest? And less than 42 per cent of people in the UK bothered to vote at the last election.

So, what are we really talking about here? Ultimately we're talking about *your opinion* of yourself being the one that counts. It's that simple. You're either pulling your own strings or someone else is. It's your tune or someone else's. You're living a life of your own design or someone else's. This is beyond liking yourself, though that's a vital part of it. This is about backing yourself. 'Walking the talk'. Getting real about yourself and your life. This is about slaying desperation once and for all. Not being needy/neurotic ever again, neither of which is the least bit attractive anyway, whatever you've been taught.

Making your opinions matter begins with taking the decision that this is how it's going to be from now on. It's a new rule in your personal handbook. Now you need to observe it, remind yourself to keep it. Every time you feel yourself slipping into needing someone else's approval, respect or liking, pull back. Take command of yourself. Remind yourself that you no longer need to do this as you approve of, respect and like yourself. It's a dynamic choice with far-reaching effects. This doesn't mean that you turn into a monster who never challenges themselves or changes their mind. It means that you think *independently*. It means that you reach your own conclusions and aren't afraid to make them public. It also means that, when criticized – it happens – you 'front up'. You handle it head-on. You decide how much of it is justified, whether there's a case for you to answer. If yes, you act decisively to remedy the situation. Then you move on, without agonizing or tormenting yourself. If, after due reflection, there is no case, then you defend yourself appropriately, perhaps vigorously. If the situation is not black and white, then it's a judgement call – your judgement. Get used to backing yourself in this way. It gets easier with practice.

Internal composure and strength depend on healthy self-reliance. Self-reliance gives you definition, a glowing, honed, self-contained look. Self-reliance is the real mark of a successful relationship. And there's none more meaningful than the one you're having with yourself. It'll run and run. There's just no end to it. You're with yourself for all time. You've just got to be able to rely on yourself, fall back on yourself, know that you can be relied upon, share the good times and the bad times. Digging deep inside, looking to *yourself* to pull yourself together will deepen your relationship with yourself. This is your opportunity to lean into yourself and come through under your own steam. Challenges build psychological muscle. Difficulties test you. You'd be dull without them. This is when you find your depth. Flex those muscles and you'll make yourself strong, confident and resilient. You walk around with less fear in your psyche because you'll have learned how to handle yourself and life. You've proven your mettle to yourself. Even if only *you* know, it'll still show. There's more to you than meets the eye. You'll carry yourself differently. You'll look as if you know things and live an interesting life. You'll look intriguing. It's called charisma.

I'm not suggesting that you give up sharing issues and dilemmas with trusted friends. There is a time for this. But most of us pick up the phone too quickly. Our reflex is to look outside rather than inside. I promise you, all the answers you want you already have. You just have to ask – yourself – and you'll receive your answers. Intimate relationships will be easier and more fun. There's nothing more off-putting than a needy, clinging partner. Far more desirable is one who is perfect without you. They're with you because they want to be, because you're so darned special. You bring much added value, your own brand of specialness. Looking to someone else to make you feel good, important and loveable is problematic. Don't fall for love songs of the 'I'm nothing without you' variety. The best relationships work when you're not looking for sticking-plaster security.

Self-approval means you don't have to work overtime to make people like you. You're really, really OK with yourself. You're smart enough to know that not everyone will like you. You don't *need* them to because you're already doing that for yourself. Outside compliments are lovely but they're treats. You can't rely on them for regular sustenance. You won't grow tall on them alone. Sugary treats are highly addictive. As soon as the high wears off you need another fix to feel good again. It's not a sensible way to live. Real growth food has to come from you. You nourish yourself with every thought you think, every word you utter to and about yourself. Make sure it's pure quality, otherwise you make yourself weak. You have needs that no flattery can reach, gaps that lovers' and friends' kind words can't fill up. The solution is to seal up those gaps, wounds, and gaping holes yourself. Do this with your thoughts, words, decisions and actions. Know that only you can do this. It doesn't work to try to ingest it from outside yourself. You can only get this big, grown-up stuff by generating it from within. It's all internal, but it shows on the outside.

GET REAL

1. *Inspire yourself.*

You need a Sondra in your life. You need to see real people in action close-up. Find one and take every opportunity to be around them. They don't need to mentor you. Their presence will be enough. Identify real people in public life. In the UK think: Germaine Greer, Tony Benn, Margaret Thatcher, most 'Old' Labour politicians, Prince Charles. In the US: Colin Powell, Oprah Winfrey, Martin Sheen – on- and off-screen, Steven Spielberg, Shirley MacLaine, Ellen Degeneres, Madonna, Whoopi Goldberg, Muhammad Ali.

2. *Challenge yourself.*

You have to do this for real. It won't work otherwise. Give yourself opportunities to practise self-approval, self-reliance, self-respect. What does 'liking yourself' look like? Take five minutes to fill out three separate lists: 'What my life would be like if I approved of/ respected/liked myself more'. Then, conscientiously introduce these changes. You have nothing to lose and everything to gain.

3. *Don't argue.*

When you have reduced your dependency on others, they have less of a hold over you. You don't need them to agree with you. You don't need to win people over. You feel no urge to be right. You have no points to score, nothing to prove. A relaxed espousal of your position is one thing, a heated debate quite another. The difference lies with the emotional charge – a relaxed espousal has little, a heated debate lots. Arguments rarely change anything as the opponents dig their heels in to maintain their position. Most people so need to be right.

And some people love arguing. They get to prove themselves in this way, especially in front of an audience. You don't!

4. *Hold back.*

Resist the urge to pick up the phone. Is a problem shared a problem halved? No, that's not necessarily true. Never, ever ask for advice – or offer it. Advice is what people would do if they were *you*. They're not. What they're really saying is what *they* would do in that situation. It's irrelevant. It's you we're talking about here: your situation, your feelings, your decision. Only you will live with the consequences of your actions. Have a discussion with yourself before you open it up to anyone else. You might not need to call anyone after all. Think of the savings!

5. *Enjoy yourself.*

You can't be self-possessed unless you've come to love your own company. Can you show yourself a good time? Do you know what fun is, or does that depend on having company? When was the last time you took yourself out to lunch, a film, the theatre, a day in the country or spent Saturday afternoon in bed with a good book? That's not sad. That's fabulous. It's cool. Martha Gellhorn, one of the twentieth century's finest war reporters and ex-wife of Ernest Hemingway, said 'There's no greater pleasure in life than being on your own in bed, reading and eating a peanut butter sandwich.' Luxuriate in your own fine company. Go on, spoil yourself! And get very discerning about whom you share yourself with. You can afford to be choosy.

Keep it real.

12

More Power to You

I'm rapidly coming to the conclusion that we humans are all very similar. I believe we all share pretty much the same desires. I reckon that under all our skins is a desire to be powerful. It's a funny thing, power. It can do the most awful things to people or rather they do the most awful things with it. It's definitely powerful stuff. What is it the Anarchists say about it – 'power corrupts and absolute power corrupts absolutely'? I should know, I was one of the ones saying it! In those days I was surrounded by people who shunned money, society and status. In other words, power. On reflection, you could say that they didn't trust themselves to handle it, so they avoided the whole rigmarole altogether, opting instead for a separate, alternative lifestyle. There's nothing wrong with that whatsoever. For myself I preferred to move out, back into the bigger world, the main-stream, and take my chances. And now here I am about to urge you to be more powerful. Isn't life grand?

This is exactly what I do with individuals and organizations that I work for. I work to make them bigger, better, more powerful versions of themselves. When I take on new clients I ensure that they're people I want to empower, to have more power within themselves and in the world. That's quite a responsibility. The world won't thank me for making its monsters more dynamic and effective. There's absolutely no question that what I do and what I'm going to share with you here works. It works to make people 'big', much more powerful, which is tremendous when these people are a true force for good in the world. With these individuals I push them to be powerful and drop their self-doubt by reminding them of the immense value their position and visibility has to offer. The bigger the challenge, the bigger the opportunity to get their message across, to make their contribution. It's always worth remembering that if the good ones among us don't take up positions of power, then others less scrupulous certainly will.

You must feel the same way about yourself as I do with my clients in order to realize your full power. You must feel compelled to drive yourself on, to push yourself to whatever heights stretch out in front of you. You need a clean bill of self-worth to feel clear and comfortable about being powerful. Otherwise, I promise you, you'll hold back on pushing yourself forward. This is because we all know that power is, well, powerful. So, if you're the least ambivalent about yourself, you'll restrain yourself about being 'more', being bigger than you are now. Have a look at the 'Let it Go' and 'Be Good' chapters if you need to. Power also has something of a bad press. It's easy to think of disastrous examples of vast wealth, fame, success – all power, rather than positive ones.

We all know that a sudden rush of power can go straight to the head, throwing you off balance. I watched someone recently go from a perfectly lovely person to a monster because of a huge surge of power. All that happened was that he made a lot of money in less than a year and at twenty-seven he wasn't grounded enough to handle it. He wasn't sufficiently earthed and the massive jolt of power threw him. He'll probably recover in a few years. And there are countless showbiz stars and dotcom millionaires who burn and crash early and fast. None of this is a reason or excuse for you to shirk the challenge of bringing forth your full power.

Allowing yourself to be powerful is a challenge. Drive, ambition and the desire to achieve have brought us our greatest inventions and achievements. The car you drive, the home you live in and the plane or boat you'll take your holiday on all came from one person's drive and power. It's put men on the moon. Without it we'd still be using a horse and cart to get around. Where would we be without the powerful drive of Buddha, Jesus, Mohammed, Martin Luther King, Nelson Mandela, Emily Pankhurst and the hundreds of other lesser-known heroes and heroines whose contributions have made all our lives better, even possible?

I urge you now to take up this challenge. Decide now to go for it, to do yourself the service of being powerful. This isn't about shoulder pads, strutting around trying to impose your will on others, making all around you small so you can feel big, though people do still behave like that. That's not true power. That's not your way. True power doesn't sit on your shoulders. It isn't crude, noisy or uptight. True power is internal. It has its home deep within you. It's an inextricable part of who you are, woven into the fabric of your person. You don't put it on; it's not for show. It's under your skin. It goes where you go. You never leave home without it.

What I'm really talking about here is you growing up, and into yourself. Like everyone else, you came into this world with your own little bag of talents. You are pure gold. You're pure potential. How you use your gold is how you use your power. Truly powerful people use themselves really well. They spend their gold; they make the most of it. They don't keep it hidden from prying eyes. It's out there. They're out there, living on the edge of their potential, firing on every cylinder they were given. Are you? Are you being the best possible version of yourself? Have you settled for something small because it's easy, safe and available? Are you selling yourself short? Assume with me that you have about 30 per cent more growing still to do, more potential, more power dormant within you. Right now, ask yourself what this would look like. What would change in your life, in you, if you were 30 per cent more powerful? Don't make this difficult. It's simple. Make a note of five profound differences and we'll come back to it later.

Before I deal with the practical plan for bringing more power to you, I want to ensure that you know what you'd do with that extra clout, what the point of it would be. It's a lot easier if you have a clear reason for forging ahead. There has to be a sense of purpose to it all. Power is a bit lost without a good cause. It must have a clear focus and channel. Most companies today have a mission statement – a succinct statement that describes what the company stands for – its purpose. This simple statement provides a quick reference point for whether a decision or action fits, whether it's 'congruent'. Life is more straightforward when you have a sense of your own purpose. It puts your life into a context, gives it a greater meaning, a sharper focus, a sense of urgency. Spiritual teachers emphasize the importance of identifying that purpose and manifesting it in the world. Caroline Myss, the best-selling author of the *Anatomy of the Spirit*, talks of us all having a sacred contract. She argues that before birth we each 'contract' with heavenly guides to become vessels for divine power and evolutionary change. Whatever you make of this, you'll find it immensely empowering to decide that you are here for a reason, to see yourself as having an important role to play, bringing out your potential and contributing to the whole of life at the same time. The good news is that divining your purpose needn't involve a trip to an ashram, or a week's silent retreat, though both make fine breaks. Your strengths and talents and what you love doing are the biggest indication of where your purpose lies. As the mystic poet Rumi said, 'Everyone has been called for some particular work, and the desire for that work has been put in their heart.'

Answer these simple questions with ten words or a short statement for each:

1. What do you want most out of life?
2. What do you want to see happen in the world?
3. What makes you special?
4. Things I can do/am capable of doing right now.

Now write this statement as follows: '*I will* . . . (choose one answer from 4), *using my* . . . (answer from 3), *to accomplish* . . . (answer from 2), *and in so doing achieve* . . . (answer from 1).'

This really works. It reveals effortlessly what really matters to you. From now on, maintain your life in this context. The more aligned you are to your highest desires, the more power you will pull through yourself and express. Your motivation is of the highest order. You drive yourself to be your most powerful, most dynamic, most effective. This is pure gold.

MORE POWER

1. *Get yourself.*

Do you 'get' you? Do you get how great you really are? As soon as you do, you are instantly bigger, taller, brighter, more full of yourself. Make a list, 'Reasons to feel immensely proud of myself'. Jot down three things that come to mind immediately. This list tells you how brilliant you already are, how accomplished, how clever, how downright brilliant. Unless you appreciate your worth and value in this way, you can't use it or make it work for you. It's as though you've banked all these riches without making them grow or even buy anything useful. Impress yourself. Have a growth spurt in less than five minutes. Losing sight of yourself is easily done in a busy schedule. But the key to more power is appreciating your value. I want you to make this list so good, so thorough, so darned compelling that you swell with pride at the sight of yourself laid bare. Fill up, fill out with respect, rise up in your own estimation. Focus on that list every evening for a week. Increase in stature day by day. Get the habit of regular appreciation and admiration for yourself. This isn't an indulgence. It's a way of looking at yourself that gives you access to your own power base. The stronger you are within, the more it shows on the outside. Your power and poise is then written all over you. You're fabulous. Get you.

2. *Be discreet.*

Keep more of yourself to yourself. Powerful people talk less. They don't gush. They don't try to steal the limelight. They don't need to perform at parties. They're well aware of their position and status. They don't crave trophy girlfriends or boyfriends. They don't plan their entrance. They're not trying to impress. Which is exactly what makes them so impressive, enigmatic and, yes, powerful. Don't ever bare your soul. Resist the impulse to reveal so much of yourself. It'll leave you with the feeling that you've sold something you should have kept. You're not selling anything. You're far too priceless. Keep it that way.

3. *Don't fight.*

It's undignified. It's just not something that sophisticated people do. Winning is far more intelligent. Arguing, sulking, battling is drama. Drama queens spend their whole lives doing it. It's a full-time job.

Powerful people have bigger agendas. They honour their energy and guard against spillage or waste. They give drama a wide berth. You need to keep energy in reserve for those occasions when it's worth making a stand, taking up a position. Winning is the point. Make your point with grace and charm. People don't mind being won over. It's being defeated that they object to. Sometimes you win by walking away, or even running. Moving on may be the powerful thing to do. The power in any negotiation belongs to the one prepared to walk. Resist being desperate about anything. Prepare yourself mentally in advance. Know that you can live without this thing, person or whatever. You can! You're far more powerful than you think.

4. *Be a VIP.*

Are you important? You decide. Act as if you are. Forget about other people 'taking away' your power, 'overpowering' you, 'making you feel small'. That's absurd. People can only have your power if you give it to them. Watch yourself in everyday situations. Why hang about in a trendy restaurant for a table at the mercy of an uptight maître d'? You're pumping them full of their own self-importance and power while you languish at the bar. Having been one of those snooty maître d's – a few years back – I never wait for a table now. There's always somewhere else happy for your custom. Don't buy into this exclusive, hip, 'happening' stuff. Queuing, longing and waiting is bad for the spirit. It diminishes you. Go round the corner to a restaurant that's glad to see you. Watch yourself. Have standards.

5. *Take yourself seriously.*

Don't demean or denigrate yourself. Don't set yourself up to be a joke figure or overlooked. Take yourself lightly, but seriously. If you're the vice-president of the company, make sure *you're* the last to arrive for a meeting. Don't be kept waiting. It's not appropriate to your position. Your role is served by you taking it seriously. Behave like a vice-president or whatever your role requires. Be powerful. It's a choice. You know what the difference is. Look at the list I spoke of earlier – the five profound differences that being 30 per cent more powerful would bring. Just for fun – what differences would an additional 50 per cent bring? It's interesting. Now decide what's going to change. If I watched you over the next week, how would I know you were operating more powerfully? Be absolutely clear. Because the only person getting in your way is . . . you. You've got to watch yourself!

And finally, I hand you over to President Nelson Mandela and his inaugural speech:

'We ask ourselves: "Who am I to be brilliant, gorgeous, talented, fabulous?" Actually, who are you not to be? You are a child of God. Your playing small doesn't serve the world. There is nothing enlightening about shrinking so that other people around you won't feel insecure. We are all meant to shine as children do. We are born to manifest the glory of God that is within us. It is not just in some of us; it is in everyone. And as we let our light shine, we unconsciously give other people permission to do the same. As we are liberated from our own fear, our presence automatically releases others.'

More power to you.

13

It's All Down to You

Life's as easy or as difficult as you make it. Think about it. We all know someone who shouldn't be as happy as they are, but they are. Why are some people so light-hearted when they're not thin, wealthy, blissfully married or have an inheritance to look forward to – all the things that are supposed to make you smile? How come? What's going on? Their internal world seems at odds with their external one. And why are there some folk with every kind of worldly advantage who make such heavy weather of their lot? They can be downright miserable. It's an attitude thing. But it's more complex than positive thinking. *They're* more complex. They make it that way.

Caroline came to see me to figure out her next move in life. She had cover-girl looks, was effortlessly skinny and comfortably off, with two gorgeous little boys and a lovely home. I'm sure you get the picture! Yet she was miserable, and complex. Her burning desire was to write novels. This was entirely appropriate as both her parents were successful writers and she had previously worked in journalism. 'Simple enough,' said. 'Figure out a plot, employ me to keep you on track and off you go!' Well, it works for everyone else. Caroline came up with the most bizarre reasons as to why she couldn't just crack on and get the words done. Here's a sample: her parents were so successful that she felt overshadowed by them; maybe she had no real talent; maybe there was something else she should be doing; maybe this wasn't the right time. Best of all, she concluded that her comfort denied her the hunger that would really pull that novel out of her. She figured that if she had been a single parent living on benefits, she would be better off because she'd have real motivation. I reminded her that many people don't use this situation as motivation, finding the cushion of benefits comfortable enough or utterly demoralizing. How complex is it to use everything in your life and turn it into a disadvantage? That's heavy.

Sometimes seeing what you're up to is more difficult to spot. On paper everything in Vicky's life looked good; at thirty-four she was living the good life in Switzerland with a loving husband and three adorable little girls. Yet, boy, was she resentful! My first impressions of her when we met were that she seethed with resentment and was seriously suppressed. It was written all over her. Here's why. Her complaint was that she felt she had drifted through life, missing out on creating an impressive career for herself. She had left school early, taken A levels at night school and obtained her business degree later than most people. She had then had three children in quick succession and was in danger of turning her frustration and resentment on them.

Vicky felt her problem was that she had had such a bad start in life. She blamed her parents. At thirty-four, she still believed it was all their fault. Don't laugh. This is so common it's unusual to find someone who isn't holding his or her parents to blame for something. I had an e-mail yesterday from an elderly gentleman who said that his father's influence had been holding him back for over fifty years and his father has been dead for twenty of those. In Vicky's case she felt that her parents could have been much more encouraging and interested in her school life. Nothing was going to progress dramatically in her life until she let her parents off the hook. In particular she blamed them for the late start to her career, which had never really got off the ground. So, while her career languished she could make them suffer, though I'm not sure they really got the message. But *she* definitely derived deep satisfaction from showing them what failures *they* were as parents.

In addition, blaming them took the heat off *her*. She could have been fabulous, if only. She could have been on top of the world, if it hadn't been for them. There was not much personal responsibility going spare here. Luckily Vicky was sufficiently fed up with her status quo to allow me to coach her to move on from this swamp in that first session. She resolved to take more pride in her appearance, dress more flamboyantly and take total responsibility for getting the career of her dreams. Funnily enough, it was completely different from her original career in banking. She admitted that her dream was to work in television.

Blame, bitterness and resentment have dire consequences. They don't just give you an ulcer. They set up a whole chain reaction in your life. They imprison you. They literally dictate your circumstances – you can't have a terrific life because then you'd have nothing to complain about, be bitter about, no one to blame, nothing to regret and cry over, no one to punish. In order to punish someone, you need to suffer, or look much maligned. It's a complex web we weave sometimes. In this scenario there's no real winner. The accused gets on with his life, probably in total oblivion. He may even be dead. The accuser, on the other hand, suffers on, feeling blighted. And blighted they are. And they will continue to be so until they unravel what they're up to and choose otherwise.

Stay with me here. The theme is taking total responsibility for creating your life – it's all down to you. Therefore, blame and excuses of any description have to be challenged as well as the attitude that fosters them. Even if you feel you're pretty relaxed about everything, it's worth taking a few minutes here to run a check on your willingness to see yourself as truly in the driving seat. Feeling that the course of your life really is all down to you is a huge liberation and source of power. Taking total responsibility for *everything* leaves you lighter and more freed-up than the average person. Without passing judgement, listen to people; listen for their excuses, blame, justifications and resignation. They may be everyday gripes – nothing too heavy – but it all adds up to a lessening of your own power and sense of responsibility. Because you aspire to be the best, the average holds no appeal.

So, are you as freed up and liberated as you could be? Are you carrying any excess weight? Are you as lean, as light and as lithe as you could be? Let's have a look. Take five minutes to ask yourself:

1. Do I blame anyone for the circumstances of my life?
2. Is there anyone or anything that I resent?
3. Is there anyone that I need to forgive, for anything?
4. Whom do I still hold a grudge against?
5. What do I regret?

This line of enquiry may give you some interesting answers. Write these questions down, adding names and insights as they occur to you during the day. Letting go and forgiving people doesn't change the past, but it changes its hold over you. You change your response to what happened. You choose a response that frees you from the past and cuts the ties. You put it into a perspective that allows you to bury past history and make your peace with it. Otherwise you could be haunted by demons that hold sway over your life today, giving power to the past to hold you back and keep you down. The difference between heavy and light people is the habit of apportioning blame. Light, liberated people don't 'do' blame. They don't carry around baggage from their past and they don't accumulate it in their present life. That doesn't mean that they've simply led a heavenly, blessed existence. It means that they see things differently. They're more freed up because they're not dragging around grievances and old wounds with them. They travel light. One of the quickest routes to doing this is to adopt a philosophy that liberates and empowers you.

Seeing yourself as the driving force in your life is a choice. How far do you want to take this? How about all the way? Back to the very beginning and beyond. Why? Because it's far more empowering than seeing yourself at the mercy of random events and meaningless coincidences. Your life deserves more meaning than this. How about accepting that everything and everyone in your life has been there for a reason? What reason? You decide. However challenging, however awful some of the people and situations you've encountered, they have all made you bigger and better than before, potentially. Try this on for size: what if you came to an agreement before you were even born as to how you could develop and evolve yourself during your forthcoming lifetime. Free will and destiny coming together to let you bring through your strengths and talents. So, before birth, your soul is designing all of this, setting up the order of your physical life. Obstacles, dangers, disappointments – they're all perfect opportunities, they're lessons for greatness. You've scripted all of this beautifully to stretch yourself to serve your own personal and spiritual evolution. Discovering the power of forgiveness, for example, means that you will have circumstances and opportunities to practise forgiveness. How you handle your circumstances is always down to you. You always have choice and choices. If this sounds dramatic, it has profound implications as well.

It's easier to be at peace with yourself, with everything that's ever happened, if you can make sense of it and derive benefit from it. Look back at any person or situation that you're uncomfortable with. Now see it from this perspective. What was the opportunity, discovery, lesson and great strength you could pull from that time? It's all there to be garnered and used for your advantage. The aim is to resent or blame no one so that you squeeze every last drop of value from all your experiences.

Goldie is a graffiti artist, hip-hop icon, DJ, actor and all-round international star. He drives a Porsche, a Mercedes and a BMW. He shops at Gucci and lives in a mansion in the Hertfordshire stockbroker belt. He parties with other musicians, hobnobs with Bowie and Björk, poses on catwalks in London and Milan and played the baddie in the Bond film, *The World is Not Enough*. At thirty-six success looks easy for Goldie. However, he has spent much of his life conquering his own troubled childhood. His father left soon after he was born. His mother put him into care when he was three. He remained in a succession of institutions and foster homes until he was sixteen. Goldie has talked about his upbringing, recently taking part in a Channel 4 documentary on his life, which featured his mother, father, old foster-parents, teachers and other ghosts from the past. When asked about happiness he said this: 'Life in general makes me happy. The one thing I've realized, out of everything, is that I'm a lifer. I'm a person who has seen life, enjoyed it, and hopefully passed some of it on. That's all that really matters to me – passing that life vibe on.'

Goldie's real success isn't his lifestyle — it's his life. It's the fact that life threw so much at him so early and he just kept on handling it. His real triumph is to have kept himself light. He could be bitter. He isn't. He could so easily be miserable, justifying it brilliantly. He could so easily hate the world, feeling it owed him. His life could so easily have turned out so differently. At sixteen he left council care to find his mother and live with her again. He remains close to her today, dedicating one of his most famous musical pieces, 'Mother', to her. When asked if he's proud of everything he's achieved, he says, 'Most of all I'm proud of all my friends for sticking by me — the people that stood there and that are still there.' His immediate response is one of gratitude, noticing what he has got to be thankful for. That's light.

DOWN TO YOU

1. *Grow up*.

Divorce your parents. Thank them for *everything*. Once you're over twenty-one their primary job is done. From now on it's down to you. Let them off the hook. Absolve them of future responsibility. You're taking over, taking total responsibility for creating the life that you want, for being your own person. They may not like it. So be it. It's better to live with a little disapproval than a lifetime of blame and regret. That's the price of responsibility and the mark of maturity. Your prize is freedom. Freedom to live a life of your own making. You don't have to be cruel but you do have to cut the cords to separate and really grow up.

2. *Lighten up*.

Don't be heavy. Cultivate lightness. See good in everything. See opportunity everywhere. Appreciate sun, rain, sleet and snow. Life's as easy or as difficult as you see it. Make it easy by keeping yourself light. Watch your interpretations. A late train gives you time for coffee. Flu lets you catch up on all that daytime TV you've been missing. Watch what you make of everything. Keep it light.

3. *Be grateful.*

An attitude of gratitude takes you from victim to victorious. It sets you free from the past. See yourself as privileged. See your upbringing, school, and friends as pros not cons. Never ever wish for anything different. You're missing the point, not getting the benefit. What's your edge? Public school, state school, posh or poor, whatever. What have you got, experienced, seen and learned that sets you apart? It's there for you to see. Turn everything to your advantage. Don't miss a thing. Lament nothing. Embrace everything.

4. *Choose your choices.*

Accept that on one level or other, you chose and choose everything in your life. What's the reason, the lesson? Get conscientious about your choices. You might want to choose different people or situations next time. Don't make the mistake of blaming yourself for your choices. Above all, don't moan. Powerless people moan. Victims whine. That's not you. If you do feel the need to moan – you're human too – do it consciously, to someone who lets you get it off your chest, for no more than fifteen minutes. Then move on. If you've got serious complaints, do something about them.

5. *No excuses.*

Check that you aren't harbouring any festering grudges, any what ifs or if onlys. Anything that would get in the way of you taking 100 per cent, absolute and unconditional responsibility for creating the life that you want. Be rigorous. You can't afford to waste a drop of your precious energy and life force. You need it all. Giving great chunks of your power away to the past or having it tied up in resentment and blame is not a good use of it. Muster everything you've got. Don't look back. No regrets. Front up. Onwards. Always.

It's all down to you.

14

Get Motivated

Motivation is the Holy Grail for self-help experts. Gurus, sages and philosophers down the ages, across generations, have all been searching for the key to unlock motivation. Motivation is the master key to all success. You achieve little without it. It's the engine, the pump room of your desires, dreams and ambitions. It's the bridge between passion and action. You won't go far without it. It drives you into action. It's good, it's destructive. It's powerful. It's whatever you make it. It'll take you anywhere, to do, be or have anything. You have just got to have enough of it. Thankfully, you can have as much of it as you like. You just need to know how to make it and keep it.

I've read a lot on motivation. I've watched people who have it and people who don't. The individuals I've been drawn to and admired the most have had lots of it. I like driven people. They definitely bring a certain urgency to the table, to their lives and everyone else's. They're powerful people. Energy and drive are incredibly attractive. They are seductive. They are downright sexy. They lead. They inspire. People follow, feed off them, draw strength from their force. And all because they have motivation, clarity, passion and drive. It's an awesome power to have. These people rule the world. They always have done, they always will. They wage wars, lead revolutions, overthrow governments. They're despots, dictators, saints and saviours. They have the power to persuade us to take to the streets for good or evil. It's the purity, the clarity, the unswering conviction that makes them so compelling and irresistible. Think Bob Geldof and Live Aid. Who will ever forget the pure passion and drive of the man? Old ladies pawned their wedding rings, multinational giants handed over thousands and politicians were whipped into action. We were all affected, inspired, moved and motivated. The world felt small and we came together. On that day Bob Geldof ruled supreme. No wonder he's been Saint Bob ever since, however reluctantly.

The power of motivation is indisputable. People behave differently when they're motivated. A football team, a sales team, an army, a nation, a school, a family: they're all transformed when motivated. Smart companies know the value of motivated staff. High company morale keeps people, keeps them happy and it's good for business. A UK firm was recently featured in the national press with headlines like, 'How a hug in the office can help to triple profits', 'The office where the boss gives you a hug.'

The engineering company, Farrelly Facilities & Engineering, fosters a caring philosophy in which overtime is forbidden, soothing music is played and the fifty employees are banned from working on their birthdays. Since the loving philosophy was introduced three years ago, the company has seen profits and productivity triple. The company had pottered along for ten years until training manager Gerry Farrelly began studying Eastern philosophies such as Tao Te Ching. 'The results have been amazing since we decided to take this path. We find by creating this easy atmosphere the workers respond by giving their all. Profits are up by 200 per cent in the past three years.' Adam Boyce, a project engineer, has been with the company for six months. 'I have worked for a few mechanical firms and found them to be the same. But it is different here, we are made to feel a part of the team, we are pushing in the same direction. I wouldn't swap this job for any other, even if I was offered a lot more money. The quality of life here is much more important to me.' This last comment is the most intriguing. Money isn't the key motivator.

Warren Buffett is one of the world's wealthiest and most successful business leaders, whose net worth is estimated at $30 billion. His role at Microsoft is to motivate a team of fifteen to twenty managers, to keep these key people enthused about what they do when they have no financial need to do it whatsoever. 'At least three-quarters of the managers we have are rich beyond any possible financial need and therefore my job is to figure out how to cause them to want to jump out of bed at six in the morning and work with all the enthusiasm they did when they were poor and starting.' Bill Gates started Microsoft with an investment of $1,500. Today Microsoft's annual sales exceed $14 billion.

Motivation is so powerful that you'd think it must be obvious to companies everywhere. Not so. More than 60 per cent of employees in the UK are demoralized by their jobs and a further 20 per cent do not care about work. Most staff are happy to do the least necessary to keep their jobs and they just go through the motions, dispirited by the nine-to-five grind. Demotivated workers drain capital from businesses and cost the UK economy between £339 billion and £348 billion a year according to a recent Gallup survey. They blamed poor management techniques for the lack of interest shown by staff in their jobs. The report concluded that bosses needed to encourage a culture in which staff feel wanted and that they have some value to the company and its future.

Feeling valued, feeling part of something, feeling that you are making a worthwhile contribution to something important is a common theme here. And money may have absolutely nothing to do with it. I saw this for myself during the 1980s. At that time huge weekend American seminars were all the rage in London. Every Friday evening London's hotels would swell with hundreds of eager folk keen to sit in a hotel room until late Sunday night making sense of their lives. It was great. I loved every minute of it. The big ones were the Loving Relationships Training (LRT), the Forum and Insight. The organization of these events was awesome. At the Forum in particular, you'd step out of the underground to be met and greeted by clearly marked 'assistants' welcoming you, directing you to the hotel. All along the way were more assistants. You stepped inside the hotel and there was more of the same. It was a military operation, brilliantly planned, immaculately executed. Nothing was left to chance. Motivation of the highest order was at the heart of it all. Pure clarity, clear sense of purpose, total conviction. Not one of these 'assistants' was paid a penny. Yet they carried out an impeccable job of service to ensure that we, the participants, had the best possible experience. Think of it. Captains of industry on toilet duty! Their commitment to the success of the seminar was excellence in the area of hygiene. They were delighted to make their contribution in this way. Why? Because they fervently believed in the power of that seminar to make a massive contribution to the quality of people's lives and, in turn, to the entire planet. It didn't matter whether they cleaned toilets or served tea. It all served a higher purpose. They went home in the early hours of Monday morning with a profound sense of achievement and contribution. Perhaps more so than they ever did at work. Money alone could never have bought the service they provided.

Your success depends on how strong your level of self-motivation is. It's not discipline that moves mountains or lifts a car to free a trapped child. It's not discipline that lets you drop ten kilos, give up smoking, take up running, set up your own business, save the planet. It's motivation. Survivors of life-threatening illnesses usually have phenomenal self-motivation. I want to demystify motivation for you, simplify it for you. I will give you a foolproof plan to follow. It works. It's the best of everything I've ever read, learned and seen, distilled into a simple format. Do it and you can have as much motivation as you want, and keep it. Then life is much more straightforward. You won't fight or struggle with yourself. You can be highly motivated whenever you choose. You'll feel directed, compelled to act in line with your objectives. Self-motivation makes getting up at 6.30 for your pre-breakfast run so much easier.

I want you to know precisely how to turn up the heat on your own desires, drive your passion, feed your longings to get the results you want. I want you to grasp the simple mechanics of motivation so you can flick the switch to turn on, turn up your own motivation whenever you need to. Having the ability to generate your own motivation internally is vital. Mentors, trainers and coaches can reinforce and lend you theirs. Ultimately you need your own to succeed.

Dropping weight is something most of us are familiar with. I've been fat and I've been thin. I've been your average couch potato and I've run races. I've had personal trainers, gyms, classes, fasts, detoxes. My observation is this. None of it works – necessarily. Yet any of it can, once you've handled your own motivation first. In fact, personal trainers can make matters worse. They can't work magic. I've seen fat people stay fat, with the services of a personal trainer. I've done it myself! Right now, I'm getting great results with a trainer. Why? Because I want to, really, really want to. I worked on my motivation *before* working out with him. Cindy, Elle, Naomi and the rest do not have great bodies because they have the best trainers in the world. They just have better motivation than everyone else. Think about it. If you're shooting your next film in six weeks, which literally millions of people will watch, that's quite a motivator. Or you have a new exercise video to film in a month's time: that definitely helps to focus the mind.

Mentors are invaluable, if used well. Charles came to me looking for a mentor. He said the times when he really triumphed in his life were when he had a great mentor, at school, on the sports field, in his first job. Without them, life was flatter. I offered my services to Charles as a coach, but not a mentor. This is the distinction. Charles looked to his mentors to motivate him, to drive, push, coax and cajole. Without their spurt, he had none of his own. He didn't know how to flick the switch and generate his own. I coached him to mentor himself, to motivate himself, so he didn't deflate without outside injections. He learned how to get himself impassioned, focused, driven, compelled to take action.

Anthony Robbins is one of the greatest teachers of personal development. His theories about motivation centre on how we use pain and pleasure: 'The secret of success is learning how to use pain and pleasure instead of having pain and pleasure use you. If you do that, you're in control of your life. If you don't, life controls you.' This makes a lot of sense. If you've ever been in a job that you loathe, or a destructive relationship, and finally decided to take action and do something about it, it was probably because you'd hit a level of pain you weren't willing to put up with any longer. We've all experienced those moments in our lives when we say, enough is enough, this *has* to change, now. Successful slimmers often say the turning point for them was when they saw a holiday snap of themselves and were so shocked by the sight that their resolve appeared as if by magic. Their moment had come. This is the moment when pain drives us to change our lives. It's vital to learn what creates pain for you and what creates pleasure. You can obviously influence this by training your mind, body and emotions to link pain or pleasure to whatever you choose. With smoking, for example, all you must do is link enough pain to smoking and enough pleasure to quitting. Anyone who has successfully quit will have changed what smoking meant to them. In fact hypnosis does exactly this. It conditions the mind to attach negative emotions and connotations to whatever you want to cut out, whether it's chocolate or cigarettes.

GET MOTIVATED

1. *What's your pain?*
   Right now, what could you use to trigger your motivation to push you towards action and change? Is there a habit, a situation, a job that's got so bad that it's close to unbearable? How bad would it have to be for you to leave or change? You can intensify this feeling, and therefore your motivation, by focusing on the cost of staying in this situation. Ask yourself this question: 'What will this cost me if I don't change? How does another year, five years, of this look and feel to me? What would I miss out on by not changing anything?' Make the pain of not changing so real that you can't put off changing any longer. If it's smoking, confront yourself with the cost to your health and life expectancy by speaking to someone who's had a limb amputated, or heart surgery or lung cancer as a result of smoking. Look at the prematurely aged face of a forty-year-old. Avoiding a similar fate for yourself will reduce the appeal of cigarettes instantly. Use this clarity and intensity to move *away from* what you no longer want. Recovering alcoholics use the pain, the

memory of their addiction, to keep them highly motivated. They never want to go back. The pain outweighs the short-term pleasure of a drink. Recovery programmes serve as a reminder. Avoiding pain is an incredible motivator.

2. *What's your pleasure?*

While avoiding pain can move you *away from* what you no longer want, focusing on what gives you pleasure, *towards* what you want, is a more long-term motivator. Once you've dropped the weight, or your breathing's recovered from twenty cigarettes a day, you need a different motivation. Your original motivation might have to be replaced with a desire for a taut, sculpted body, stamina to run races, looking younger, feeling more attractive, having more energy, whatever inspires you. Strong motivation needs what Robbins calls 'leverage'. To paraphrase the philosopher Nietzsche, he who has a strong enough 'why' can bear almost any 'how'. Twenty per cent of any change is knowing *how*; but 80 per cent is knowing *why*. In other words, when there's a will, the way is easy. If you gather a set of strong enough reasons to change, you can change in a minute something you've failed to change in years. To convince yourself, to drive your desires in the direction of change, ask yourself this question: If I do change how will that make me feel about myself? How much better will my life be if I made this change today?' The key is to get lots of powerful reasons to make change irresistible. You change because every fibre of your being, every cell, every muscle desires it. You become a person possessed with inspiration and enthusiasm. Onlookers envy your discipline. They're wrong. It's pure motivation.

3. *Have a vision.*

Get motivated by the spectacle of a terrific life in front of your eyes. What does this look like? Where do you live, with whom? What are you doing? Go on, let yourself get excited. Take your passion out to lunch. Just you and your longings. Whet your appetite for the changes and improvements you'd like to make. Savour every detail. Take your time. Divide it into categories for the different areas of your life, financial, physical, social, career, family, travel, spiritual. Soon you'll take on the appearance of someone who's going places. You've seen the future, and it's fabulous. You've got things to look forward to. Be inspired. It's crucial. Your enthusiasm, optimism and vitality will draw to you the very things you desire. Passion is power. Make it work for you.

4. *Believe it's possible.*
Suspend judgement. Choose to believe that your desires are entirely possible. This is *you* we're talking about here. You know that if you want something, anything, badly enough, you get it. You've done it before. Remind yourself right now of something that you wanted so much that you got it. You have unlimited motivation at your disposal. It's there waiting to be put to good use any time.

5. *Enjoy yourself now.*
Appreciate what you already have and strengthen your desire to attract and create success. The secret of personal success is to be true to yourself and to continue to want more. When you really want more, you'll get it. Wanting more and appreciating everything right now lets you have it all.

Relax. You've got the will to succeed. You're on your way.

Get motivated!

15

Get Going

People often ask me what the single most important tip for success is. That's easy. Here it is. Do more. It's that simple. Your actions define you. Success comes to those of us prepared to take action. The willingness to take action is far more important than talent, as naturally talented people will tell you. Talent is never enough. Gutsy people get ahead. Things fall into place for them. Not everything works out exactly to plan, but they always win through. They're irrepressible. They never stay down, even for a minute. They just love to be up and running again.

Being gutsy, 'ballsy', is open to all of us. There's no secret that I'm about to reveal to you, or maybe there is. It's simple. These people take action, regardless of how they're feeling. They don't wait for a full moon. They don't wait for a better time. They definitely don't wait until they feel better about themselves, whatever that might mean. If this sounds a bit simplistic, it's because taking action, getting things done, achieving more is very straightforward. You do more, you get more, you have more, of whatever it is that you want. The secret is, there is no secret.

When people come to me for coaching, they generally know what they want. I ask the same question of everyone: 'What have you actually done about this so far?' I'm not being critical. I'm being curious. The answer? For the vast majority of people, it's 'absolutely nothing', or as good as. Very occasionally someone will say, 'Everything. I've done everything. Nothing's worked.'

I can work out a terrific plan of action with people. I can increase their confidence, inspire them, intensify their motivation, build them up, make them more powerful. But I can't make them jump, take the steps, make it happen. Only you can do that. It doesn't even matter how confident you're feeling. If you don't do the necessary, what you know needs to be done, nothing will change. You certainly won't make the gains that you could. Don't make the mistake of thinking, 'If only I had more confidence, then I'd get things done.' It doesn't work like that. There's no substitute for plain, old-fashioned action. Just get on with it.

A client, James, illustrates this perfectly. He is a leading men's health expert, and his dream is to set up a cutting-edge integrated men's health clinic. It is a tremendous concept and he was the man to do it. He was already taking action, was well on his way, but he was also taking every opportunity to stall, procrastinate and waver. He was waiting for something, a final burst of confidence, to reassure him that he was doing the right thing, that all would be well. When we looked at it, his confidence was sky high, his motivation and sense of purpose were all in place. The missing link was action – consistent, dynamic, decisive action. There were three obvious steps he needed to take to move his plan to the next stage. He was the only one stalling and the only one who could move things forward. All that stood between him and a monumental leap forward in his life were three simple steps. I could do no more than stand aside and cheer him on as he crossed the line. He would have to jump with his insecurity still in place. And he did. He crossed the line between a thinker and a doer. He turned himself into a man of action. His confidence, his estimation of himself, soared overnight, in a way that no amount of talking or chanting affirmations could have done. Don't wait until you're perfect or you feel absolute certainty. There's nothing like making things happen to feel invincible. You can sit at home writing affirmations for years – some people do – and nothing much will change. You need to get out, get to grips with the world, do business, engage, make things happen, take chances, get it wrong, have a go.

Some people read books and spend vast amounts of money and most of their lives at seminars, learning to improve their lives. What life? There's nothing left after the workshops and seminars are booked in. I've seen this close up way back in the late eighties when I did a lot of weekend seminars and courses. I noticed that after a while everyone looked the same. That's because they were. The same people 'sharing' the same 'stuff', the reasons why they felt stuck in their lives. They even seemed to cry at the same bits. I know this sounds cruel, but it's really true. Seminars, lectures, a few great books and tapes are an invaluable way to keep positive and meet new people. I'm a great believer in continual self-improvement. But doing repeat weekend courses, thirty days here, ten days there, takes up a lot of time. You might even get to think there was something wrong with you, which the next course could fix. No one's perfect. Life is for getting to grips with, rolling up your sleeves and getting stuck in. Studying the theory is all very well, but it's no substitute for the real thing.

That's why I love coaching. It's about results, taking action. Talking will get you so far, but it's action that counts. Quite often people get into the habit of talking and that's as far as it gets. You can talk yourself into things and out of things. Never, ever sit round a kitchen table talking about what you really, really want to do. Have that conversation with yourself.

Get top-quality support if necessary and get going. Get on with it. Talking too much takes the edge off your resolve. Take action first, talk later. It's not healthy for people to see you as a talker. You'll start to see yourself in this way. Walk your talk. Demonstrate what you're made of. Don't discuss it.

Right now Russell Crowe is the most wanted actor in Hollywood. Oscar-winning star of *LA Confidential, Gladiators, A Beautiful Mind*, he's made it. I saw him interviewed recently when he was asked about ambition and success. He said that he had kept his desire to act tucked away inside him from about the age of nine onwards. He told no one. He took action instead. He just kept on doing the right thing, showing up, practising, getting parts, learning, getting better. He felt that to talk about it, to discuss his ambition was a waste of energy that would dilute and undermine his focus and drive. It felt far too important and precious to put on the table for discussion. Right attitude. Right actions. It's an unbeatable combination. You cannot fail to succeed.

Knowing when to take action and when not to is an art form. There is definitely a time for pushing forwards and a time for holding back, biding your time, waiting for people or things to come to you. This is not inaction. This is action management. You've already put things in motion, you've sown the seeds, and now you have to be a little patient. Wait for your efforts to bear fruit, develop, return. Trust your instinct. But be absolutely honest that this is what's happening. Ask yourself if there's *anything* else you could be doing to move things along. If there really isn't, pull back. Decide how long you're prepared to wait. Sometimes you initiate action that doesn't bear fruit for years. It looks like an overnight success, but you know that it's the result of action you took years earlier. Other things have a shorter timeline for momentum and completion. Delay, and the moment has passed. Opportunities come and they go. Which ones do you grab? It's your decision. The more you're in the habit of taking action, the more you're in this flow, the better your judgement.

The worst place to be is right at the edge, poised to take action, holding back on doing so. You've drummed up your motivation, you're feeling good, everything's in position. Yet you hold back. it happens to the best of us. The only solution is to just do it. To do the very thing you know you need to do. Yes, you could discuss it some more, again. Review your motivation, again. And then, all that's left to do is to do it. Make the call. Say yes, say no, whatever. Just do it. Follow through. The alternative is more talk and excuses. Staying immobilized is downright depressing. The best antidote to everyday depression is activity. The Oriental saying, 'This too will pass,' means this very thing. Rather than search inwards for answers, the answer may lie in looking outwards, in activity, in moving on. Your salvation lies in greater action, more engagement. Looking inwards to move forwards may keep you even more glued to the spot.

I admire people who pick themselves up from their lowest point and live on, from a broken heart, a disastrous love affair. How easy it would be to shut down, contract, withdraw, say no to everyone for ever. To put yourself out in the world, choosing to cheerfully go forth is brave, fabulous and, in some cases, downright awesome. To get knocked down and get up again is truly impressive. There's no alternative to getting right back up on that horse again before you lose your nerve, never to gallop or jump again. Sometimes more action, more effort, more of the same is the only remedy. Ask yourself right now, is there anything you've withdrawn from, given up on, decided you can't have, resigned yourself to never doing or having? If so, when did you make that decision? Just notice that you made a distinct choice that involved a stepping back from and out of life. I see this quite often with people who have demanding careers and work incredibly long hours. Work is something they can excel at, whereas intimate relationships may be something they've given up on. The likelihood of a relationship happening is therefore scant, because they do nothing to create possible opportunities. The people who have success in this area put the work in. They're out there actively looking; their friends are doing the same; they're checking out dating agencies, the Internet, throwing parties. It's only a matter of time, and effort, before the right person materializes. I've seen it happen in a few weeks. Yet other people don't manage it in twenty years.

If action isn't bringing results, pull back. If you keep on doing things the same way, you'll get the same results. Question your methods. Is there another, a better way of achieving your objective? Avoid getting fixated on the means. Your ultimate goal is the point. Adapt, change direction, cut your losses. Admit what's not working and why. Don't be afraid to admit you got it wrong. Stay on top of it all. Action for action's sake is a waste of time. I've seen bankruptcy looming and people are frantically occupied, going nowhere fast, refusing to stop and see. Like anything else, you can use being busy as an excuse for not facing up, changing direction, making decisions. Action serves you when it's the right action: premeditated, focused in the right direction and getting results.

GET GOING

1. *Be a doer.*
What have you done for yourself lately? Think about something you'd like to change, improve, achieve in your life. Without being critical, simply ask the question: 'What have I done about this?' Do your actions suggest real commitment? Are you really serious about this? How much do you want it? What are you prepared to do to demonstrate real commitment? If you were one of the most dynamic, fearless people in the entire country, what actions would you be taking?

2. *Get results.*
Are you being effective? Being busy is not enough. Time is precious. Are your actions economical, directed? Are they working? Be honest with yourself. Don't get too busy to stop and ask if you're heading in the right direction. Are you a perfectionist? Crack on. Don't let it stop you. Prioritize what's worth the extra effort. Experiment with less effort. Some things benefit from a lighter touch. They're fresher.

3. *Embrace uncertainty.*
Don't put off getting going until you're absolutely certain. It may never happen. Get comfortable with 80 per cent certainty, reminding yourself that the only certain thing in life is – uncertainty. The more you jump, walk, run with uncertainty by your side, the less of a handicap it feels. You get used to it. Experienced men and women of action know it's part of the process, at least at the outset.

4. *Be decisive.*
Decisions, decisions, decisions. Love them. Choose fast. The less you agonize, the more you decide, the better you get. Practise being freed up around decisions. Don't think wrong/right. Think conse-quences. All decisions have them. Not all decisions are equal.

Cappuccino, mochaccino, americano, whatever. Just decide. Fast. Never, ever tell yourself you're hopeless at making decisions. Act otherwise.

5. *Do more.*

Unless you're a spiritual master living at the foot of the Himalayas, the smartest way to have more, of anything, is to do more. I appreciate that the likes of Sai Baba may well have the knack of materializing physical objects out of thin air, but it could take you and me a lifetime to get the hang if it. It's probably faster to work with the reality we have on our doorsteps, that of taking action. When we do, miracles often happen; the universe meets you halfway. As Goethe said, 'Whatever you can do or dream that you can do begin it. Boldness has genius, magic and power in it. Begin it now.'

Go on. Get *outta* here!

Get going.

16

What Do You Want?

Knowing what you want and going after it sounds straight-forward enough. So far, so simple. We all have greater opportun-ities, freedoms and choices than ever before, especially women. Social mobility means anyone can go anywhere. We're not excluded from anything because of our accent, school, gender or background. We can access all areas. Post-war affluence and a welfare state means we'll never starve. Yet we're less happy, less fulfilled and content than we were fifty years ago. Depending on which survey you accept, a 25-year-old is between three and ten times more likely to suffer from depres-sion than someone of that age in the fifties. Why are many of us more depressed and dissatisfied than fifty years ago?

The global online careers site, Monster.com, recently ran a poll across Europe called, 'How did I get here?' Results show that less than a quarter of Europeans are happy in their chosen careers, with 78 per cent admitting to having drifted into their current position. Only 22 per cent of respondents consider themselves to be either working in or towards their career goals. In the UK and Ireland only 3 per cent of us feel we're in our dream job and we work longer hours than anyone else in Europe. We're too busy making a living to get a life.

What is going on? Sociologists say it's because of our raised expectations. We want more. We're more demanding of ourselves. We want more out of life. It's true that we have far greater freedom to have what we want. We live in a world with the possibility of having everything and being anyone. Our choices are endless, opportunities are unlimited. That's an incredible freedom. Feeling the world open up to you can feel intoxicating. It can also feel too much, overwhelming. No limits, no boundaries, no excuses. Freedom can dazzle you, stop you in your tracks. Where to turn? What to go for? Getting it right, it's your choice. There's no turning the clock back, no return to the simpler life of fifty years ago. It's all too easy to romanticize the past. Life might have been easier because it held fewer choices, fewer opportunities, more restrictions. Handling the world as it is now, without seeing freedom and choice as a burden, is the way forward. It's the big challenge. It's tough to know what you really want when the choice is so vast, but it's a problem worth having. We should be so lucky.

Figuring out what *you* want when you're surrounded with other people's ideas can be bewildering. Advertising and marketing people are some of the smartest people around. Their job is to persuade you to want exactly what they want you to want, to inflame your desires so much that you're driven to have that car, that drink, those shades. 'Search for the hero inside yourself' while you're having 'the drive of your life' in a Peugeot 406. Buy a L'Oréal colour conditioner because, well, you're worth it. The Mazda MX-5 Phoenix 'is the only place to be seen if you want to stand out from the herd'. Meanwhile the McDonald's 'M' logo is the most universally recognized symbol on the planet. Success is living in the fast lane, earning six-figure salaries, yearly bonuses, second homes. Postcodes define you. A bigger car for a bigger you. Simplistic, I know, but you're surrounded by all of this. Your wants are being meticulously planned for and sketched out right now. Buying into it isn't a choice. Opting out of it is. Finding your own way through, figuring out what you want, is probably harder than ever. The pressure to want what you're conditioned to want is intense. The 'culture' of *Hello!* holds up airbrushed pictures of perfection as the route to all happiness. *People* magazine and the *National Enquirer* in the US do the same. Designer homes, designer lives. If you buy into this stuff you could easily feel yourself falling short by comparison. Would you feel like a 'loser' if you wanted something different? Are you so busy keeping up, making a living, that you might be missing out? Back in the past it was the norm to loathe what you did for a living. The real you emerged at the end of the day, the week, to come alive again. You returned to your real self, to do the things you really wanted to do. Work was something to be endured so that real life could be maintained. Not any more. Now, we want more. We expect to do meaningful work that allows us to express ourselves at the same time. This is a raised expectation and a great one at that. Work has to work for you. You want more from it than a livelihood. If you're dissatisfied, it's because you know there's more to life. And you want it.

Living the life you want is likely to add years to it. Dr Rosy Daniel, former medical director of the Bristol Cancer Centre, says, 'Becoming inspired and committed to life and doing things you love is what makes the shift in the body's ability to heal itself.' Nowhere is the mind – body connection more graphically demonstrated than at Bristol where, using a holistic approach, hundreds of patients facing the prospect of death made dramatic changes to their lives, sometimes with astonishing results. 'There would be a huge unlived life sitting there and when people were given permission to live it, it was like a match to a touchpaper,' recalls Dr Daniel. 'But they all wondered why they had to be so frightened before making these changes.' Do you want what you have? Do you know what you really want? Of course you do. No question. No doubt. You may not be clear right now. It may lurk just under the surface, but, trust me, trust yourself, it's there. You know.

Occasionally people will feel an overwhelming sense that they're living the wrong life for them, that they took a wrong turning at some point. They're just not cut out for it. This could be true. Recently *Cosmopolitan* magazine asked me to coach a few readers for their Valentine's Day issue. Naturally, the focus was their readers' love lives or lack of them. One of the girls, Jackie, felt totally dispirited about life in general. I wasn't surprised. She just didn't fit into her life. She was too big. It was too small. It happens. She was a gorgeous 25-year-old who had been a singer on luxury cruise ships for the past few years. She loved this but felt she needed to 'settle down'. Back to dry land in London and a job in an estate agent's, so far, so utterly miserable. I resisted telling her she'd got the wrong life – that's not my job. She was smart enough to see this for herself. Don't get me wrong. Selling houses is great if that's your thing. Jackie was just the wrong person. Twist and turn as she might, she was never going to make it fit.

I had only one session with her, which left her with more questions than answers. Four months passed. A week ago I received an invitation to her wedding. Apparently after our session she accepted that she didn't really know what she wanted next in life. But she definitely knew what she didn't want. With that knowledge she headed back to what she loved, singing. During her first week back on the ship she attended a lecture given by a young man on motivation. Ten days later they were engaged! I'm off to the wedding in four weeks. Sometimes you have to give yourself a shake, get a change of scenery, take time out of your life, freshen up, blow away the cobwebs. Jackie was lucky in that she only had herself to consider, but there are heaps of people equally freed up who stay stuck. Sometimes you just have to up sticks and see things differently.

People live in denial. They deny the truth even to themselves. Why? First, it means so much to them. It's risky to expose the truth. Nobody wants to be laughed at, especially when something is close to your heart; far better to conceal it. Second, you might have to do something about it! Once you reveal what you really want, even to yourself, the truth is out. You've just 'outed' yourself. The genie's out of the bottle. There's no going back. You either move forwards or feel even more dissatisfied than before.

Your passion, your enthusiasm, your heart's desire is *already* a part of your life. There's no mystery. It's so much a part of you, it can't not be. Take a look at yourself. Look at your book-shelves, your free time, evenings and weekends. Look at what you're intrinsically good at, what you're already doing. I remember asking a new client what it was that she really wanted. She protested that she had no idea not a clue. I asked her to tell me what I would see if I paid a visit to her home. What would stand out? What would strike me immediately? Straight away she said, 'Cookery books, books on food, the history of food, first editions, modern writers, they're in the kitchen, bathroom, downstairs toilet. I've had extra shelves specially made to hold them.' I simply said, 'Thank you, I get the picture.' Eighteen months later she's poised to open the most fabulous food emporium in the centre of London. Surprise, surprise.

Sometimes what you want isn't about wanting more of everything, but less. I came across this story the other day in the *Daily Mail*. At fifty-two, Richard Snow travelled the world business class, no expenses spared. Richard was an executive with Standard Chartered Bank with a six-figure salary and a fabulous home in the Surrey stockbroker belt. But for Richard it had become a 'continuous slog', leaving little time for life outside work. He has just given it all up to be the village postmaster in a small village in East Yorkshire. One week into his new life and Richard has no regrets. 'It's a different lifestyle. Here we're part of the community. We're very enthusiastic about what we're doing and we're going to make a go of it. The only thing we miss about London is the traffic!' Richard had to give up everything to have more of what he wanted.

The secret of a happy life is to do more of what you enjoy. Know what you want and act on that knowledge. You'll be happy, loving what you do. From that comes all the energy, talent, ideas and actions to achieve success. We're never good at anything we don't really enjoy, so you have to find something you want, something you enjoy, something you can throw yourself into.

WHAT DO YOU WANT?

1. *What don't you want?*

What do you no longer want in your life? What no longer works? This should be straightforward enough. What do you no longer want to tolerate, put up with, say yes to? Sometimes having more of what you want is only possible when you say no to what you don't want. List five things you definitely *don't* want. Clean up, clear out. Make room for something better. Remember that what you wanted three years ago might not be what you want at present. Life moves on. You might want something different now.

2. *What have you settled for?*

What have you given up on that really matters? One of the saddest things is to change what you want, rather than what you do, to accept things that you never really set out to get in the first place, whether a lifestyle, a standard of living, an income, the lack of a social or love life, or having no time with your family. Have you compromised on things that really matter to you rather than learn a new way to go about things? Choose one thing that you need to focus on, one thing that's worth the effort. Admit it's important. Take it down off the shelf. Don't give up on it, or you.

3. *What do you really want?*

Answer this question: 'If you knew you couldn't fail, what would you do?' Go on, you know you know. Don't worry about the 'how' part at this point. Give yourself the gift of five minutes out of your life to play with this question. Look at yourself. Stand back. Look through the keyhole at you, your life, from a distance. What stands out about this person? What's glaringly apparent about the intrinsic nature of this individual, their passions? What sorts of books and magazines do they have? What sort of a life would you expect this person to be living? Are you living it? If you're not sure whether something really is that important, ask this question: 'If I did nothing about this, how would I feel looking back at the age of seventy-five?' If it doesn't really matter, you don't want it enough. If it does, you do.

4. *Do you want what you have?*

The grass isn't always greener. Constant craving makes you a good consumer. More things, different people, more holidays may be more of the same. There's nothing wrong with wanting the best, but you may already have it, for now. Single people want to be married. Married people want to be single. These might be your best years right now. Don't wait for hindsight to tell you so. Stop and think. What's really great about your life right now that you don't appreciate, or even moan about?

5. *Choose your influences.*

Select your conditioning. Garbage in, garbage out. What are you filling your head with? Pull back from looking at all celebrity magazines for at least a month. These perfect people are the ones most tormented with self-loathing, eating disorders, drug and alcohol abuse. Don't buy into the illusion that they have it all and you're the onlooker. You're better than that. Your own life is far more interesting. Guard against wanting what ad men need you to want. This season's 'most-wanted' fringed bag or 'must-have' 'folk-chic' look will be 'so over' so soon. A man no less than La Rochefoucauld put it well when he wrote a few centuries ago: 'It is by having what we like that we are made happy, not by having what others think desirable.' Looking good, loving fashion is one thing, but draw a line. Fringed bags have 'victim' written all over them.

And remember. If you don't ask, you don't get. Now,

What do you want?

17

Get What You Want

I used to loathe the idea of planning. I loved feeling I was a free spirit. The notion of setting goals made my blood run cold. Goals were for wimps. Nerdy, business school types did that. I'd far rather go with the flow, let life come to me. Going out to get it was far too contrived for someone as cool as me. But then I was twenty, well, twenty-five. But it's never too late to get a grip. And that's how I see the whole area of setting goals and planning. Getting a handle on what you want and having a plan. In other words, taking your life and yourself seriously.

In my work as a coach I've seen too many people who've left their lives to chance, who've drifted, ending up thinking, 'How did I get here?' As a result they feel that life has passed them by, forgotten about them. Their wishful thinking becomes wistful. People can get very disillusioned at this point. It's all too easy to give up, turn to clichés like, 'Oh well, it wasn't meant to be', 'God has something else in mind for me'. Very occasionally this may well be the case. But I can't recall an example right now. Some get bitter and look for something to blame. The truth is they never had a plan in the first place. Or it was so wishy-washy that they wouldn't know whether they'd arrived or not, having had no particular destination in the first place. Either way their spirit is diminished, their enthusiasm sapped. They reduce their wants and expectations, resigned that life has less to offer them. Resentment and envy can creep in. Observing this close up alarms me. It's put me off drifting.

Maybe it's something to do with not being twenty or twenty-five any more, but I think life's a bit short and too darned important to leave it to chance. Taking a risk on getting a table at your favourite restaurant on a Friday evening is one thing. Hey, it's great to be spontaneous sometimes. But not with your entire life. And why should God have to do all the work? We're here for a reason, to make a go of things, get on with life. Let's get serious.

I don't mean heavy, grim serious. I mean taking yourself seriously. Don't you want a fabulous life? Of course you do. Is your life important? Definitely. Are you worth it? You bet. Let's get busy. Let's plan and scheme. I can't bear to be bored. I loathe hardship. The journey has to be first-class all the way. You've got to enjoy yourself as you go, otherwise it's dull. We don't want that. Pursuing dreams, having goals has to make life more interesting right now, not just in the future. Think how much fun you could have if your goal was to find a husband or a wife. Exactly.

Goal setting has had a bad press. So few people actually have clear goals. Even fewer have clear, *written* goals. It's something that other people do. I think this has something to do with presentation. The whole process is a bit foggy, a bit dreary, complicated. Another reason people don't set goals – and probably the most important reason of all – is the fear of failure. Lacking faith, you do not believe in yourself sufficiently to have the very thing that you want. So, not even bothering to try in the first place means that at least you can't fail. Suspend all of that for the moment. I'm going to make the process of setting goals simple, straightforward and fun. It doesn't have to be a struggle and it mustn't be dreary.

Do you know where you're going? What direction are you

heading in? North, south, east, west? Life's not called a journey for nothing. We're all leading somewhere. But where? You'd never set off on a long trip without knowing where you were heading. It'd be strange not to have a route mapped out in your mind and probably on paper as well. As you go you might even change direction slightly, altering your course depending on how it looked as you got there. But you'd know what you were up to, what you were about. You'd definitely know if you arrived.

I no longer think goals are for wimps. I know different now. Goals are for all of us who want an interesting life and are prepared to do something about getting it. Strong-minded people set goals. Why? Because they believe they can achieve great things and they don't mind putting the effort in. That's confidence. It's optimism and go-getting and putting yourself out there – and on the line sometimes as well. It's looking on the brightest side and being utterly pragmatic at the same time. It's wimpy to be otherwise.

People who accomplish great things are often dismissed as 'lucky'. In other words their achievement, their good fortune happened almost by accident, by divine intervention. Look closer. You'll find a plan, every time.

A year ago David Edwards became the first man to win £1 million on British TV's *Who Wants to Be a Millionaire*. The day after his appearance David revealed his meticulous campaign to win. A Physics master, David knew he had enough general knowledge to answer the fifteen questions he would face. The real challenge was to get onto the programme in the first place. He worked out that he would need to dial the show's premium rate phone number up to 1,000 times to guarantee a place within six months and so he set aside £1,000 from his £26,000 salary to pay for it. To his amazement, it took only twenty calls to get his first appearance on the show. However, blind panic let him down as he fumbled with the keyboard during the 'fastest finger first' section when contestants have to put dates or names in order. Undaunted, David came home and reapplied himself to taking another chance. He made many calls and also practised punching in numbers – 'I did it until I didn't have to think which finger was button "B" and read question cards from the quiz's board game.' Finally, after spending £300 he got his second, ultimately life-changing, chance, 'I went into it thinking I had a realistic chance of winning a large amount of money. It was slightly cold-blooded because I thought if I could get six figures, it was a chance to retire early and do the things I couldn't do with my commitments and two children at university.'

David was certain he could do it. He just needed a chance and he wasn't leaving that to chance. Since David's win, there have been other millionaire winners. Each one revealed a plan, as precise and focused as David's. There was nothing random about them either getting on the show or winning. The first female winner, Judith Keppel, ran up such a phone bill getting onto the show that British Telecom called to warn her that teenagers must have been using her phone.

Philip Beresford, Britain's foremost expert on the rich, says the difference between the rich and everyone else is simply this: 'We can all talk up a good idea in the pub, but 99.9 per cent of the population never does anything about it. A money-maker will get up the next morning and, even with a massive hangover, have the confidence to turn that idea into a money spinner.' As Body Shop founder, Anita Roddick, once said, 'Business isn't rocket science.' Great ideas require a great plan. They have no real value until you do something with them.

If you're serious about getting anywhere, achieving, anything, you've *got* to have a plan. The best sort is written. Here's why. In 1953 a group of Yale University graduates were asked a key question: 'Which of you has written specific goals?' Only 3 per cent of the group had clear, written goals. Twenty years later, in 1973, the group was revisited. The 3 per cent who had written goals had accumulated more wealth than the other 97 per cent added together. This example has often been quoted to demonstrate the phenomenal power of the written word. Think of the advantage you give yourself by putting pen to paper.

The reason we're going to set goals is to give our lives focus and to move us in the direction we would like to go. Remember that what you focus will increase in your life, and you become what you think about. As the spiritual guru Wayne Dyer says, 'You are what you think about all day long.' Even if you did no more than write down the direction you'd like your life to take, you'd benefit enormously from the enhanced mental clarity. You'd have a psychological advantage. Your mind would be consistently pulling you in that direction. But, of course we want to follow thought with strategy and action. In a moment we'll get to grips with a plan.

But there are two things we need to do before that. First, it's worth reminding yourself of your values, your purpose. If you haven't carried out the purpose exercise from the chapter 'More Power to You', please do so. Your goals and plans must come from your highest, clearest motivation. Your actions must be in alignment, congruent with your personal values and priorities.

Second, what's your dream life? Let's put aside the 'how' for a moment. If there were no limits, no boundaries, what would your life look like, where would you live, what would you do? If money were no object, if you didn't have to work for a living, what would you do? Let yourself get excited. Write this out in five minutes or less – a paragraph will do. This is for your pleasure. It should lift your spirits, fuel you. Now write a sentence declaring why you deserve this. Smile. Let's get going.

GET WHAT YOU WANT

The Rules

1. *What would you do if you knew you could not fail?*
Think about it. If you were absolutely confident of your success, what would you want to do? What actions would you take? Be specific.

2. *Are you passionate?*
The stronger your desire, the more likely you are to act on it. Emotion is energy in motion. The fear of disappointment can make you hold back, reducing the full power of your intention. Fight it. Let your longing propel your actions. Only choose goals that really matter, then bring the full force of your intention to the operation. Paradoxically, resist feeling desperate, insecure or rigid. Leave yourself open to the possibility of your goal materializing in a form other than you can imagine right now. Don't cling. Otherwise you're limiting the way it can come to you. Affirm, 'I am ready to receive this or something better.'

3. *Choose to believe it's possible.*
The moment you declare what you want, all manner of doubt can show up to throw you off course. Head this off by anticipating it and dealing firmly with it. Affirm positively to yourself statements like, 'I now take total responsibility for creating the results I want in my life', 'I now believe I'm good enough to have the life I want, I deserve to be happy.' You are the master of your thoughts. Choose to believe in your own potential.

4. *Relax.*
Go within. Build the habit of meditation; fifteen minutes of pure silence stills your mind and disciplines your internal world. The more

stillness you have, the greater clarity you bring to your world. Deepak Chopra says this links you to infinite creativity, the field of pure potentiality. You will effortlessly receive your most creative ideas and inspiration from calming your internal turbulence. Begin by ensuring you have a quiet, private space where you won't be disturbed. Lying down may encourage you to sleep. Sitting comfortably is best. The object is to simply allow your thoughts to pass by without holding onto any. At first you may have ideas and thoughts vying for attention. Keep a notepad by your side so you can jot anything down. With a little practice this will happen less often.

5. *Visualize your desired outcome.*
Contemplate; see in your mind's eye what you want to bring to fruition. First thing in the morning, last thing at night, see yourself in the best possible light, moving seamlessly through your day or experiencing your particular goal. If it's your dream home, see it in vivid detail, outside, inside, every room, furniture, objects, everything. Map out your intentions on a 'treasure map'. Find pictures of what you want to achieve and draw to you, and arrange them on paper. Display the map where you'll see it every day or carry it with you.

THE ACTION PLAN

1. *Write everything down.*
Buy an A4 notepad for this sole use. Give yourself headings for each area of your life: career, finances, family, social life, relationship, health and fitness, spirituality. Add any others of your own. Use fresh pages for each heading, so it's easy to see at a glance. Now go over the list and estimate when you expect to reach those outcomes: six months, one year, two years, three years. I find anything beyond three years loses its urgency.

2. *Prioritize and plan.*

Now is the time to move things up a gear. Choose four goals that you want to actively work on, that you can accomplish this year. Pick the things you're most enthusiastic about, whose achievement will make the biggest difference to your life. Underneath each chosen goal write why you deserve this goal. What difference will it make to your life and the fulfilment of your purpose? Now 'bless' it with this affirmation: 'I give thanks for this or something better in my life, on or before the (insert date) for my good and the good of all concerned.'

On separate sheets of paper write the goal headings out again and now break down where the goal will be in a year's time/six months/three months/one month from now. To progress the goal along as you've laid out, what are you willing to do over the next seven days? Do a weekly plan of action for each of your four chosen goals of what you are willing to do to move forward over the next seven days. Take action today on each of the four goals. This demonstrates your intent. A phone call, a visit to a gym on the way home, a step forward, however small, it's all it takes.

3. *Review and renew.*

Keep these goals active. Carry the headings of your four chosen goals around with you. Renew and update them every week. Read through all your goals and review any developments once a month. Stay open to changing direction, stepping up your activity at any time.

4. *Get support.*

Keep your goals and plans confidential. Don't share them with just anyone. Support is most beneficial. Choose it wisely. Find three other go-ahead individuals who will propel you along with their energy and conviction. Meet weekly or fortnightly and you'll be amazed at how beneficial you'll find this. There's a very good reason why Weight-watchers and AA work. Its called camaraderie. A shared purpose. One goal. They work when you attend the meetings. Your actions and resolve are fed and strengthened. Dropping weight, staying sober, to get what you want, get a group.

5. *Celebrate!*

You're on your way. If you're willing to put pen to paper and follow a plan, you've joined the elite few who do. Remember, as little as 3 per cent of the population bother to have clear, written goals. Those who do, do well. That's you. Stick with it. Your efforts will be rewarded. Acknowledge your progress weekly and at any high points in between. Don't suspend feeling terrific until the goal is complete. People who do this invariably feel flat as they cross the winning line. Enjoy the journey. Enterpreneurs, millionaires, anyone who's achieved anything they're proud of, they all invariably say their early days were the most fun. Don't miss out. Every day is valuable. It all counts.

Congratulations! You're on your way to getting what you want *and* making life more interesting right now. Enjoy it!

Get what you want.

18

Choose Success

Two years ago Kevin Spacey was Hollywood's most admired
actor. He had just picked up an Oscar for *American Beauty*,
following a run of acclaimed performances in *LA Confidential*,
The Usual Suspects and *Seven*. He was untouchable. Then came
The Shipping News. 'In *The Shipping News* Kevin Spacey gives
a performance that sinks from downbeat to almost deadbeat
. . . you may wonder what's happened to his acting . . . and
where he once jangled our nerves, at present he just grates on
them,' said the *Independent*'s critic. 'Kev has had a run of turkeys.
"He's had to drop his fee per picture by £1 million," whispers my impeccable source,' trilled the *Daily Mail* 'Wicked
Whispers' page.

How on earth does Kevin Spacey feel when he reads this
kind of stuff? How does he know who he is, how good an
actor he is after public derision like this, a universal panning
of his work? I suspect he's got this whole success/failure thing
sorted for himself to have survived so far and keep on making
movies. Otherwise he'd have packed his bags and said goodbye
to Hollywood a long time ago.

Success and failure. You've got to get your head around it
if you want to lead an interesting life. Ambitious? Get a grip
on failure otherwise it'll get the better of you – just the thought
of it. Fear of failure can stalk you, haunt you, scare the life out
of you. At the very least it'll contain you, restrain you and rein

in your big dreams, schemes and grand plans. It's so powerful it'll stop you from even taking a single step in the direction of what you desire most. It can have you in its grip without you even really knowing it's there. It contains your worst nightmare. All your worst fears and fantasies are held in its palm. Don't underestimate its power. There can be only one winner in this contest. It *has* to be you.

Your mission, and I urge you to accept it, is to face this demon, and win. I want to push you to own up to whatever fears and fears of failure might haunt you, playing havoc with your life. The enemy is within. Your demons hover at the back of your mind, waiting to show themselves as soon as you have a bright idea, contemplate a major change, take a bit of a risk. Fear of failure does not discriminate. It will attack anyone regardless of position, power or status. I've seen it take a hold on powerful, confident people as soon as they contemplate doing something different. In sport, it has become recognized that such anxiety can make top professionals turn in performances like amateurs. Extreme fear of failure can lead to a physiologically debilitating effect in the part of the brain that controls movement. The result is elementary mistakes, which jeopardize the chances of success. Psychologists call this 'choking', where well-trained professionals are reduced to making basic errors because their mind has convinced the body it's not up to the job. The trick is to know that once you are not afraid to lose, you can start to take the kind of riskier decisions that give you more chance of winning. This strategy holds good for bringing about success in any area of life.

What I've noticed is that it shows up as soon as you start thinking about something that really matters to you, of the heart's desire ilk. Or, maybe it rears its head the moment you imagine moving beyond your 'comfort zone'. This is the place where everything is familiar. You know your way around, you could sleepwalk through it, do it bound and gagged. But, hey, it's familiar. Familiar has its appeal. There are no surprises. It's safe, predictable and a bit cosy. This is the comfort zone on a good day. The rest of the time it may be more of a dead zone. You could be like a zombie in it, on automatic, going through the motions. It's easy to spot people in their dead zone. They have a vague, trance-like expression. The lights are on dimmer and there's absolutely no one home, there hasn't been for maybe years. These people live in a twilight world. They checked out; they switched off some time ago. Can they come back to life again? Absolutely. Any time they wake up to their real selves. As soon as they remember why they switched off, what it was that they said no to, walked away from. Make no mistake. The dead zone is full of people who lost the contest, or who didn't fight at all. In the battle between stepping out and giving in to their fear of failure, they lost. They withdrew at the crucial moment, settling for what they already knew, rather than stepping out to something different. Fear of failure won.

I'm describing an extreme situation. But it exists. These people are everywhere. The 'living dead' are those among us who gave up on what would have made them fully alive because they couldn't handle the thought of 'failure'. Ask discreetly and they'll give you the details of their demise, the day they gave up on themselves and resigned themselves to a smaller life, to 'the way life is'. Their justification will be other people, the competition, the economy, the timing. Occasionally they'll blame themselves, saying they just don't have 'the bottle', 'what it takes'. Or they'll have branded themselves a failure because of something that happened.

I spotted someone wearing this look a few years ago at a seminar I took in London. Jack was fifty, going on seventy. He had a look of sheer weariness, a seen-it-all-and-given-up look. He was one of the most suppressed people I'd ever seen. After a while he began to relax and look less guarded. I cautiously enquired as to whether there was anything in his past that he felt weighed him down or sapped him. He explained that fifteen years earlier his business had taken a tumble. For some time he was no longer the main breadwinner. His wife was. It took him a while to establish a new career as a financial advisor, which he had made a great success of. But he was branded. This was the only obvious 'failure' he'd ever had in his life. Perfect student, good grades, lovely wife, beautiful children, terrific life, and then failure. Or so he saw it. He'd never made a full recovery from that time. Until now. I coached Jack to see his 'failure' as anything but. He admitted that he had missed the early-warning signs that the business was in trouble. But the moment he did, he worked overtime to halt the decline. And when the collapse happened, he retrained and threw himself into a new career that was now successful. In addition, he had a fabulous marriage and was a superb father to his three gorgeous daughters. He was an active member of his church and community. In short a terrific person. A success. He saw this and as he did the twenty-five other delegates spontaneously applauded him. Jack subsequently points to that day as the moment he started to come fully alive again. He lifted off the yoke he'd been burdened with and rebranded himself. He left at 5 p.m. looking a different person, fifty going on forty-two.

Round the corner from the seminar Madonna was preparing to strut her way through one of her most successful stage shows ever, part of her Drowned World tour, years after her career nosedived following a string of flops. After box office flops *Shanghai Surprise* and *Body of Evidence* critics and many fans had written her off. What she's shown is that failure need not be the end of one's dreams. In common with many who go on to achieve power, Madonna is a classic example of what psychologists call a 'rebound personality'. Such people do not see failure as something that marks them permanently. Still less do they see it as a defeat. Instead, rebound personalities are renewed, even inspired, by failure.

Winston Churchill, Hillary Clinton, the late Princess Diana all came back fighting after a period in the wilderness. Many of Hollywood's most interesting stars have all made 'remarkable comebacks' after being written off as 'past it'. John Travolta has 'come back' so often he's known as the 'grand-daddy of comebacks' and Kevin Spacey may well have come back by the time you're reading this.

Psychologists argue that of all the triggers to success, failure and loss are perhaps the greatest. But why do people like Madonna have the ability to bounce back, while others simply allow their loss to overwhelm them? Stephen Palmer, Professor of Psychology at London's City University, says: 'People who turn failure into success blame what they have *done*, but not themselves. They see the failure as the result of mistakes they have made that are not central to their personality . . . If you actually label yourself as "a failure", it is very, very difficult to pull yourself out of whatever pit you are in.'

The difference between ultimately successful people and everyone else is not that they have never experienced failure. The difference is in their *response* to failure. Of all the possible responses to a disappointment, the worst one is to see the experience as forever determining your future. If, for example, someone you're attracted to rebuffs you, you interpret this as meaning (a) you'll never attract anyone desirable again and/or (b) you're not attractive. Because you believe things are hopeless, you stop trying and, as a result, it does indeed appear that things are as you feared. But how come the tenacious never let themselves get so downcast? The key lies in their analysis of why the failure happened. They conclude that setbacks are caused by things that can change. If it's they themselves who are the problem, they believe they can bring about a personal transformation to correct whatever the deficit might be. So, if they get rebuffed, they assume they need to improve their appearance or social skills. The successful see failure as teaching them valuable lessons about what needs to alter within themselves so that they can finally attain what they want.

This explains why so many of the ultimately successful bounce back often completely transformed. They see all success as the inevitable consequences of just finding the right button of change to press. Overcoming fear of failure in the workplace, and everywhere else, is central to success. Otherwise your fear of failing can lead to decisions that are too conservative and secure. You do things that just make you tick over. Winners dare to win. You need to remove that psychological barrier that holds you back.

Catherine Zeta-Jones has just signed a nine-film deal worth a reputed £54 million – making her Britain's highest-paid actress by far. Catherine, who joined the Hollywood elite when she married Michael Douglas, is thought to be making around £6 million per film. Yet not that long ago her career in Britain was going nowhere fast. The best roles she could get were in films like *Blue Juice* and *Splitting Heirs*, which flopped dismally. Friends advised her to join the Royal Shakespeare Company for a thorough classical training. Her reply: 'But I want to be a star.' She packed her bags and took the biggest gamble of her career, arriving in Los Angeles with nothing more than a few introductions. She says: 'There were many times I thought I was out of my mind but I persevered because I never wanted to look back in years ahead and think, 'if only I'd had the guts to give it a shot.' Catherine could have stayed in Britain and concluded that she was never going to be a star. Instead, she changed tactics by moving to Hollywood and going for broke. She didn't waste precious time making her failing career personal. She knew a fresh start was what was called for.

CHOOSE SUCCESS

1. *You're successful right now.*
   You're important, loveable, good enough. If you're waiting for the one huge achievement that will give you this certainty, prepare to wait for ever. Your worth as a person does not increase as you accumulate prizes like wealth, power, or fame. You are infinitely precious. There's not another person on the planet quite like you. You're a one-off. No success or failure can alter that fact. Value yourself now, not when you've got the bigger house, car, job. You're priceless right now.

2. *Rebrand yourself.*
   Understand, *you* are not a failure. If something doesn't work out, figure out another plan. Make failure your guru. It can teach you everything you need to know about your past and your future. Have you already branded yourself a failure? Have you made failure personal at some point? Stop immediately. You're hindering valuable insights and getting in the way of your own comeback. Rebrand yourself in the light of a more useful analysis. As Tina Brown said on the demise of her magazine *Talk*, 'There is nobody more boring than the undefeated. Any great, long career has at least one flame-out in it.'

3. *Face your demons.*
   Confront your fear of failure. Bring it round from the back of your mind to the forefront. Look it square in the eyes. Stare it out. What

exactly is its power over you? Make a list right now: 'What I fear most of all about failure is . . .' Fear of failure is better out than in your psyche running around unchecked. Once you've faced up to your demons they'll instantly lose their hold over you. Laugh in the face of them. As you rise up, they fall. You're bigger than them. Now, turn your attention to the outcome that you *do* want. Focus exclusively on the success that you desire. Each and every time a demon stirs, grab it, face it and march onwards. Do the very thing that you fear and you demolish the fear in that instant. As Seneca said a few centuries ago, 'It is not because things are difficult that we do not dare; it is because we do not dare that they are difficult.'

4. *Take more risks.*

Don't be uptight about perfection. If things don't work out, you'll have had fun trying. Check that you're not worrying about what other people might say or think about you. Are the neighbours that important? Yo! Sushi entrepreneur Simon Woodroffe has the right idea: 'If it all went wrong I could earn a living just talking about how it all went wrong.' Take more risks. No one ever got anywhere, did anything interesting, without taking risks. The question is: what's worth taking a risk on? Can you live with the risk of doing nothing and risk nothing changing? The trick is to take controlled risks. Analyse the potential benefits and disadvantages of taking action and weigh them against the potential consequences of not doing anything.

5. *Success breeds success*

But only if you notice your success in the first place. Then you can feed off it. If it's invisible to you, you can't put it to good use. You can't breed from it. Are you successful? Of course you are. Take a good look at yourself. What are some of your finest achievements?

Look at your *life*, not just the money and career. Have you ever been a great friend, partner, parent? Have you ever made a huge difference to someone? Of course you have. You're a successful *person*. Don't scupper yourself.

Remember that ultimately there's no such thing as failure. There are only actions and consequences. It's your *interpretation* that labels things success or failure. Ensure you have a *useful* interpretation of you and your life. Who says you're a success or a failure? You do. What's your label? Go on, choose. Choose wisely.

Choose success.

19

Be Happy

I used to sneer at happy people. I thought them shallow, vacuous and quite ignorant really. To misquote Morrissey, Heaven knows I was miserable then. The problem was that I felt it was my duty to be grim. It was the only way to be under the circumstances. I had no right to be happy. No one had. How could anyone smile when the world was in the state it was? We faced famine, Third World poverty, an arms race, Margaret Thatcher, Ronald Reagan, Arthur Scargill and the miners, cruise missiles in the Home Counties. Nuclear annihilation at the touch of a button. What was there to smile about? Grim-faced and weary was the only sane response.

I got more and more tired, spending days in bed. Saving the world was killing me. I couldn't see any hope for change. There just wasn't enough goodness to go round, on so I thought. I mixed with young people full of what was known at the time as middle-class guilt, sorry that they'd had such an easy time. They were certainly making up for it now. Don't get me wrong. All the causes I was involved with were entirely worthy, they still are. I'd just taken on the burden of the entire world full time and at twenty-six I felt ancient.

And then I made a decision. To be happy. Just like that. I was tired of being miserable. I came to understand that there really is something called a life urge. I found mine. I wanted to live. I wanted to be happy. It was a monumental decision because it meant everything in my life had to change. I didn't care about being right any more. I just wanted to be happy. I had to begin again, leave everything and everyone behind, take on a new identity. I was living with revolutionaries who thought my interest in alternative therapies 'bourgeois', Live Aid a gimmick and Louise Hay a raving lunatic. I had to go.

I left my old life behind and moved to a place of my own. I had a boyfriend who made the transition with me but that was it. Then the real work of getting happy began. I planned it meticulously. I read only uplifting books. I gave up newspapers for a month. I followed my interests in massage and meditation. I took every motivational course I could find. I met bright, smiley happy people, which was the biggest shock. I practised smiling. I stopped feeling so tired. I changed the way I looked and the way I looked at the world. I saw hope everywhere. I set up a massage practice and within a month had a waiting list after a magazine raved about it. I made money, ate out at restaurants and got a cat. I trained myself to think like an optimist. Then one day I noticed I felt happy. I smiled to myself recently when a journalist wrote that I was possibly one of the most positive people on the planet. It's not been without a lot of effort!

Happiness begins with a decision. You don't have to go the extremes I did. It depends on how unhappy you are. I had to take drastic measures. Hopefully you won't have to. But there's definitely a lot of unhappiness around. You can even take a course on 'How to be Happy' or sign up for a laughter workshop. Amazon.co.uk has 788 books to sell you with happiness in the title. Research suggests we are no happier than people were in earlier generations even though we have more choices, opportunities and freedom. Indeed, studies have shown that if we were born after World War II rather than before it, we are ten times more likely to feel depressed.

The very people you'd assume would be ecstatically happy are frequently unhappy. Rock stars, who must surely 'have it all' have been identified as suffering from something called Paradise Syndrome, a listless boredom and dissatisfaction that seems to come on when everything you could possibly want is available to you on tap. And Jessie O'Neill, heiress to a $350 million fortune, even offers consultations in the States (at a reputed $1,000 a day) for the super-rich who suffer from what she calls 'affluenza'. This 'condition' is exacerbated by never knowing whether people really like you for who you are or for your cash, and of having no need for structure, purpose or motivation in your life. Money buys food and shelter, and a luxurious life, but not necessarily happiness. The USA, for example, is much more affluent than in the 1950s, yet about the same numbers of people say they are happy today as compared with then.

Psychologist Oliver James has written an entire book on the subject. In *Britain on the Couch* he argues that the way we live now is bad for our mental health, that as we get richer we raise our standards and increase our expectations. Constantly comparing ourselves to others leaves us feeling continually dissatisfied. It's called relative deprivation. I saw this recently when I met a 42-year-old investment banker who lived one of those 'enviable' lifestyles. I gasped when I read her CV. It had 'Perfect Life/A-grade Achiever' written all over it. She had a fabulous house in London's Chelsea, degrees from Oxford and the Sorbonne, a housekeeper, a chauffeur-driven car to the office, the lot. Yet she talked as though she was poor. She didn't see herself as affluent. By society's standards she was a 'winner'. I asked her who she was comparing herself to and, sure enough, it was to individuals who were among the super-rich, with their own private Lear jets. Compared to them, she felt like a 'loser'. Was she happy? Not really. Even 'the most beautiful woman in the world' who married 'the most eligible bachelor' was plagued with self-loathing and an eating disorder for most of her life. The late Princess Diana may well have spent years comparing herself with too many women, leaving her feeling inadequate and insecure. Most astonishing of all, she felt fat and ugly compared to models and actresses. It was only in the last few years of her life that she came to an acceptance and appreciation of herself that gave her genuine happiness.

Happiness can't be bought in a shopping mall. That's why malls feel so soulless. Retail 'therapy' is a short-term fix, an instant lift that doesn't reach the parts you want it to. Finding the perfect shoes gives you a buzz but there *has* to be more to life than shopping. Not for a lot of people. In Britain it's our favourite leisure pursuit. Having that YSL Mombasa bag, 'the world's most wanted bag', according to the *Daily Mail*, marks you out as a 'complete hipster: you know a must-have item when you see one'. The Marc Jacobs boots or the Miu Miu wedges or whatever, set you apart, put you in the league of the fashionistas at the front row of the shows. You're in with the 'in' crowd or is it the 'it' crowd? But for how long? It'll all be so 'last season', 'so tragic', so soon. Buying status doesn't give you deep satisfaction. It's called spiritual poverty.

So if riches and shopping don't bring happiness, what does? The super-rich who stay sane are the ones aware of their good fortune, who use their fame and riches to a good end. They've found something more enduring than the pure pursuit of power and position. Premier League footballers are often in the news for their off-the-pitch escapades. Twenty-somethings earning £20,000–£90,000 a week have tended not to handle it very well. Recently, however, some have been bucking that trend.

In the past few weeks some of the game's most high-profile players have been in the news for handing over huge sums of money to charitable causes. Sunderland's Niall Quinn was praised in Parliament for deciding to donate £1 million to children's hospices; Leeds United's Gary Kelly is giving £500,000 to cancer charities in Ireland; and Highbury defender Tony Adams is donating £500,000 to Sporting Chance, the charity he initiated to help footballers addicted to alcohol and drugs. 'I've always valued other things in my life more than money. I decided to do this a long time ago . . . and the reaction I've got has really touched me,' said Niall.

Jemima Khan, glamorous wife of former cricketer Imran Khan and daughter of the late billionaire James Goldsmith, has been in the papers recently, but not because of her attendance at celebrity parties or premières. Jemima was highlighting the plight of refugees on the Afghan border who had fled drought and the Taliban. Before aid agencies and Kofi Annan of the UN had reached 80,000 people, Jemima had already visited the country twice, distributing hundreds of tents to families living under plastic sheets, and she has now set up a fund to bring tents and latrines to the rest.

It's easy to be cynical about celebrity do-gooders. For the most part I believe their efforts to be entirely altruistic. The list of the rich and famous who genuinely have a grasp on a world other than their own is impressive: Elizabeth Taylor, Pierce Brosnan, Robbie Williams, Bono, Bianca Jagger, Susan Sarandon, Tim Robbins, Martin Sheen. Their benevolence and the contribution they make give them a contentment and satisfaction that money couldn't buy. Isn't it possible that they've cottoned onto something that many people haven't – that a happy life consists of more than the accumulation of power and riches? Could this be part of the reason why people were happier in the 1950s? They had all had the recent experience of pulling together to defend themselves and others from a common enemy. The war effort had called on people to make sacrifices and concentrate on more important issues. Post-war Britain was still pulling together to build a country 'fit for heroes'. Relative deprivation was a long way off.

Spiritual masters and great statesmen are often the most cheerful of all, even when their own circumstances are anything but. Nearly every time you see the Dalai Lama he's laughing or smiling. And he makes everyone else around him feel like smiling. The Dalai Lama is probably one of the few people in the world who if asked if he's happy, even though he's suffered the loss of his country, will give you an unconditional 'yes'. What's more, he'll tell you that happiness is the very purpose of life. Western thinkers from Aristotle to William James have agreed with this idea. But isn't a life based on seeking personal happiness self centred, even self-indulgent? Not necessarily. Many surveys have shown that it is unhappy people who tend to be the most self-focused. Happy people on the other hand are shown to be more sociable, creative and flexible, and able to tolerate life's daily frustrations more easily. More importantly, they are found to be more loving and forgiving than unhappy people. Scientific evidence as well as our own experience tells us that there is an intimate connection between personal happiness and kindness to others.

In his book, *The Art of Happiness*, the Dalai Lama talks of the importance of our outlook, our state of mind, to determine our level of happiness regardless of our actual conditions. He argues that our outlook can be modified by deliberately developing an inner compassion and serenity that is unaffected by changes in material circumstances. The greater the calmness of your mind, the greater your peace of mind, the greater your ability to enjoy a happy and joyful life. 'If you possess this inner quality, a calmness of mind, a degree of stability within, then even if you lack various external facilities that you would normally consider necessary for happiness it is still possible to live a happy and joyful life.'

There are two methods the Dalai Lama favours for achieving inner contentment. One is to learn to appreciate what we already have, to make a conscious decision to be more content right now. Another source of happiness closely linked with contentment is a sense of self-worth. He argues that we are all human beings within the human community and this human bond is enough to give rise to a sense of worth and dignity. This has nothing to do with economic status and financial success.

Nelson Mandela is another individual who has the most cheerful disposition. It is easy to forget that he was imprisoned on Robben Island for nearly thirty years. When Bill Clinton met Mandela he asked how he could possibly be so tranquil and serene. Surely, Clinton asked, Mandela must still feel angry, with the need for revenge. Mandela explained that revenge was irrelevant. Focusing on the pain and suffering of those who had made him suffer, he forgave them and moved on rather than waste his energies on vengeful thoughts or actions. Happiness was his preferred choice.

BE HAPPY

1. *Choose happiness.*
   It begins with a decision. Don't put it off until you've got the perfect job, man, woman, body. Start right now to smile, to adopt happiness as your natural state, whatever your circumstances. Instead of looking for happiness, look for reasons to be happy. Cherish the

smaller moments that give you joy, pleasure and contentment. Don't take them for granted. Make them count. Build them into each day. They all add up.

2. *Be responsible for cultivating personal happiness.*

Eliminate the conditions that make happiness difficult. If you're locked into a job or relationship that you loathe, it's tough to feel happy. Resentment and bitterness make it difficult for happiness to flourish. Don't let yourself be a moaner or a martyr. Do something about it.

3. *Curb envy.*

Feeling that you never measure up, that you fall short by comparison, is bad for the spirit. Remind yourself how much you've got in your life, how much is great, compared to so many others. You're absolutely fine. There'll always be someone you could envy. Choose not to. Manage your aspirations and ambitions. Don't let them leave you feeling deprived, diminished or inferior right now. Keep a perspective.

4. *Broaden your horizons.*

Look for companionship and community. Make sure you have a gang of at least four great people to laugh and share with. Get connected to people with a common goal. Find something important, other than your career, to care about. Don't look for payment. Kindness and generosity of spirit cost nothing. The payback will be greater depth, meaning, purpose and joy for you. *You'll* be the real beneficiary.

5. *Cultivate compassion.*

Show it to yourself first before you try to share it with others. Personal happiness is your right and your responsibility. Respect yourself, care for yourself, be committed to yourself and take responsibility for helping yourself to become all that you can be. The eternally exuberant Tina Turner recently said this about happiness: 'Since I was a young child, I've been gifted with the ability to make myself happy. I haven't depended on someone else for that. I always gave a certain amount of love to myself, because it wasn't always out there, and I've never been one to draw on negative thoughts or bad memories. That's why I'm as happy as I am.' Fabulous!

Do what you have to do. But whatever you do,

Be happy.

20

Relax – Don't Struggle

Life was never meant to be a struggle. Or was it? What do *you* think? Is yours? If you think it is, it will be and if you don't, it won't. Is it that simple? I think so. Your life is the sum total of your thoughts and beliefs about life. The way life is is the way you think it's supposed to be. If you're taught that life is a struggle, then a struggle it is. One strongly held belief about the way life is can carry you through your entire life – until you see it. Then you can do something about it. Until then, life is exactly as you've been led to believe. For the most part, this is likely to be 'difficult'.

This is a widely held belief and it is certainly not new. Machiavelli is the philosopher of choice for people who struggle (strugglers). In his classic work, *The Prince*, the bible for strugglers, he wrote, 'Man is the wolf to the man . . . men eat one another.' Whilst this may have been his reality in sixteenth-century Florence, war and conflict do not have to be yours in the twenty-first. Another influential struggler, Thomas Hobbes, writing in England in the seventeenth century, is famous for the saying that life is 'nasty, brutish and short'. Present-day strugglers trot out their own homespun pearls: 'Man was born to suffer', 'You get nothing for nothing', 'You work and then you die', 'It's a dog-eat-dog world'.

Don't get me wrong. I'm not saying that life is always easy, that we shouldn't apply ourselves and put effort into things.

Life is one great big challenge that we're continually rising to. The more we relax into it and go with it, the more effective, creative and efficient we are – at everything. Picture a surfer standing still on his surfboard. As a huge wave wraps itself around him; he remains relaxed, almost motionless, letting himself be carried along by the force of the wave. If he tensed up, he'd fall. The more relaxed, focused, centred he remains, the more successful he is. It's the same with everything in life, driving your car, eating lunch, making major decisions. Struggle and push too hard and you create resistance and opposition. Struggle makes life unnecessarily difficult. With struggle, there's no joy and rarely any reward. In fact, for some people struggle *is* the reward. They're so accustomed to doing battle with life that struggle is their natural state. They're a little lost without it. There's comfort in what you know. And struggle can feel virtuous. You're being a model citizen, battling with the elements, the journey to work, work itself, everyone in it, the kids and their homework. You drop into bed exhausted but virtuous. No matter that you got no enjoyment out of much of it or that you're draining your kids. Hey, that's life, it's not meant to be fun! Obviously, this isn't you. But people do live like this. They're all around you. You could be sitting next to a struggler right now. You may have been raised by one or two. Winning is the point. Fighting and battling are not.

Josh, aged twenty-nine, came to me recently. He'd been raised on struggle. Both parents were strugglers, though his mother had since lightened up. He was incredibly successful and thoroughly miserable. On paper he looked great. Impressive CV, good grades, the right college, terrific career as a management consultant, bachelor flat in west London, future assured. But it was all such a struggle. He loathed what he did and what he had become. He could see no alternative. Wasn't this just the nature of life, of work? You just get on with it. As his father had always said, 'Hard work brings rewards.' Josh wasn't convinced.

We got busy changing Josh's life from the inside out. To begin with Josh had to grow up. At his age it was time to get his own philosophy of life, which didn't see struggle as inevitable or noble. He began to see that life didn't have to be a struggle. It's always a state of mind and reality follows on. He decided that struggle represented conflict, an indication that something was out of sync, a warning to himself. In other words, struggle was not his natural or preferred modus operandi. Then we looked at what his life without struggle would look like. It was really very easy, obvious and straightforward. So much so that he resigned the next day. Not on my advice, but once he saw how easy his life could be, he couldn't wait another minute. A month later he works three days a week freelance for the same amount of money he used to earn for five. He's taking a music course, an Italian cookery course, a wine-tasting course; he's looking for a girlfriend, making new friends, running in the park. He's got a life and he's building a future based on what's right and true for him. His biggest challenge was believing it was possible and spending Fridays doing absolutely anything, without feeling guilty, and handling his father's horror!

Do you make life difficult for yourself, more difficult than it need be? Do you create unnecessary struggle and stress for yourself? If you do, you're in the majority, especially if you live and work in Britain. According to a new report from the Industrial Society, British men have the longest working week in Europe – forty-seven hours (British women work forty-three hours). We're no more efficient and we have the highest divorce rate as well. That's a lot of struggle and it's not even productive. But then that's the nature of struggle. Growing numbers of men and women, many in their twenties and thirties, are clinically identifiable as workaholics, for whom work is the new drug. A third of fathers of young children in Britain admit to working more than fifty hours a week. The average man in the US spends just twenty-five minutes a week with his kids, yet American fathers place their children at the top of their list of priorities. In his best-seller, *The Man Who Mistook His Life for a Job*, Jonathon Lazear, a successful New York literary agent, argues that people who work to excess are just as guilty of social delinquency as the deadbeats who don't work at all.

Where did the notion of work as the central focus of life come from? The Ancient Greeks saw work as a tragedy, and gave it the word *ponos* meaning sorrow. In fact, for most of history, paid work has been sniffed at by anyone with the rank or intelligence to avoid it. Only in the sixteenth century did the Calvinists begin to talk up the notion of a 'work ethic', which was held to be both pleasing to the Almighty and improving for mankind. In twenty-first-century Japan they have a new law called 'karoshi', which means that if you die of overwork your boss goes to jail. Interesting!

We're passing stress and struggle on to our kids as well. Recent research at London's City University found 'worryingly high' levels of stress in children. 'If you asked eight year olds about stress twenty years ago, they would have looked blank. Now a significant number report experiencing it,' said Professor Stephen Palmer who led the study. The author Karen Sullivan interviewed many such children for her newly published book, *Kids Under Pressure*. She believes that children often feel stressed because parents over-schedule their lives, enrolling them for countless activities such as French and German for toddlers, computer courses and music lessons. 'Children, like adults, are expected to be busy and to be actively pursuing something for most of their waking hours. They are missing a lot of things we would associate with a normal childhood, such as being bored and messing around in the garden doing nothing.' Last year the children's charity, Childline, received 783 calls about exam stress from under-sixteens. One in seven was under the age of thirteen. At the same time, the government has introduced 'early learning goals' for children as young as three, and this generation of school children are the most tested ever. The more unhappy and dissatisfied we are, the more we want our kids to excel and do better than us.

The modern mover and shaker revels in a feverish schedule that confers status, importance and a reassuring feeling of being in demand. At the Henley Centre, the consumer consultancy that identifies upcoming trends, they call it 'stress envy', and note that high-octane living has been glamorized in television shows such as *ER*, *Ally McBeal* and *The West Wing*. But more work doesn't always mean better work. When the French limited their working week to thirty-five hours, it had the effect of increasing France's industrial competitiveness. We've all heard of Parkinson's law, that work expands to fill the time available for its completion, and it's true. Most people who work long hours tend to be unfocused, putting far more effort into things than is necessary. Over-exertion and over-delivering, not trusting enough in yourself, will make life tough. It's time consuming, draining and it doesn't even work. It won't get you the kudos you're after. It sends out the message that *you* aren't entirely confident or convinced of your abilities. Staying until 7.30 p.m. or doing a three-page report where one would do is over-delivering. Giving 120 per cent is never better than 85 per cent, because 80–85 per cent is still an A. Giving more than that leaves you looking flustered. Perspiration spells pressure.

Less would have been better. You're struggling. It might win you sympathy but not promotion.

I see this particularly with women in high-pressured careers. Trying too hard never works. Being *seen* to try so hard is even worse. It worries people. The only way to overcome this and make life easier is to stop trying to impress others or ingratiate yourself into their favour. If you're being paid to do a job, accept that you're up to it or that you'll get up to speed soon enough. Telling yourself that you're not and running to catch up is exhausting and wins you no favours. In this state of mind you're leaking vital energy by the moment. Pull back. Compose yourself. Take command of your internal state. Conduct yourself as you would if you had every faith in your ability. Remember, you don't have to know it all. In fact, there's nothing as tedious and transparent as a know-it-all. It's just someone trying to be bigger than they actually feel. That's not you. You're big enough to invite opinions, seek advice and then make your own decisions. Fearful, frantic thinking takes an enormous amount of energy, and drains the creativity and joy out of your life. You've got nothing to hide, nothing to conceal. Your identity and sense of self are entirely intact. They don't depend on an approving smile or a pat from anyone else. You don't crave acceptance, you're too much your own person for that. Don't mistake this for arrogance or aloofness, it's anything but. This is *intactness*. It's doing the job without the added complication of struggle getting in the way. Trying too hard creates stress and tension for everyone. It's not just you that suffers. Angst is infectious. Other people will catch it from you. No one wins. There's no need to do it. You're good enough, full stop.

RELAX – DON'T STRUGGLE

1. *Identify struggle in your life.*
Struggle is a programmed response so you may be doing it without noticing. Run a struggle audit on every aspect of your life, 24/7. Where have you built in struggle? Evaluate what's worth the effort and what's more of a struggle. Traipsing across town to the latest see-and-be-seen restaurant, finding a parking space and then getting back in time for the babysitter spells struggle. Is it worth it? Walking round to the local trattoria may be less glamorous, but an awful lot easier. Are you fighting with yourself? Are you locked in battle, forcing yourself to fit into a job or lifestyle that doesn't gel? Squeezing and contorting yourself to do something that goes against the grain is the biggest struggle you can give yourself. Does it really have to be this way? Strugglers would say yes. You know you've got choices.

2. *What's your philosophy?*
Are you a closet Calvinist? Do you see struggle and sweat as noble, natural or inevitable? Is it an indication of character? Are you emotionally wedded to a difficult life? Is the alternative being lazy and apathetic? If you've been raised on struggle, it may take time to reprogramme your attitudes for a more carefree existence. As struggle melts, your new positivity and inner calm pull more of the same to you. You appreciate what being 'in the flow' feels like. Let go of the idea that relaxed people can't be super-achievers. Being free and relaxed lets you see more clearly to concentrate focus and achieve your goals. Repeat often, 'The more I relax, the more I get done.'

3. *Increase your pleasure quota.*
Refine and regenerate your senses with visits to an art exhibition or a classical music concert. Pretty much anything by Mozart induces

a good mood, so whack *Eine kleine Nachtmusik* on the stereo and imbibe. Look for beauty everywhere. It may be a leaf blowing in the breeze or the sunlight on a wet pavement. Take the scenic route, not the fastest. Give yourself a break from the supermarket and shop local. Treat yourself often. Have a massage. Plan 'windows' of doing nothing – reading a novel, spending half a day in bed or an hour in the bath or watching a great video. It's all part of a juicy life. Living well doesn't require money – it's an acquired taste.

4. *Lighten up.*

Laugh more. It really is the best medicine. Bursting into laughter releases endorphins, the body's feel-good chemicals, relieves pain and boosts your immune system. You take in six times more oxygen when you're laughing, and that also makes you feel elated. The average six year old laughs 300 times a day but by adulthood the daily tally has slumped to forty-seven. Spend the evening at a comedy club. Watch a comedy video. Keep your heart light and your spirits lifted. Optimism, confidence and self-esteem depend on healthy levels of the brain chemical serotonin. Stress depletes serotonin, so keep it at bay.

5. *Exercise less.*

Strugglers make exercise hard work. There's no need. The 'no pain, no gain' approach is the way to burn-out. Over-exercising tears your body down faster than it can repair and replenish itself. If you want to lose weight, live longer and look good, go for regular moderate exercise. And it'll make you smile! Even walking for thirty minutes each day will improve your mood faster than antidepressant drugs. Exercise to the point of exhilaration, not exhaustion.

Get good at switching off. Practise lounging around beautifully. 'What is this life if, full of care, we have no time to stand

and stare?' asked the poet W.H. Davies nearly a century ago. Cut yourself some slack. You won't regret it when all's said and done. Go on.

Relax. Please! Don't struggle.

21

Think Big

Big people are everywhere. They come in all shapes and sizes. We all know one. Big people are born that way. They're like it from the outset. They have an innate, inherent bigness. It's as if they're plugged into the bigger picture without having to think about it. They have largesse, expansiveness, a broad, generous spirit. It's got nothing to do with riches or a privileged upbringing. It's all to do with character. You can breed your own. You can choose to grow your own character and spirit to enhance what you were born with; the chances are, you are a big person already.

Bigness is a way of looking at the world. It's a refusal to allow anything or anyone to diminish your size. People often contract with experience and age. They lose their freshness. They become dull, jaded, worn down. They have a jaundiced view of life and other people. They have an opinion on everything. This is not true of big people. They stay fresh. They keep themselves that way. They always look perky. It shows in their faces. That's because they're more alive than the average person. They're more vibrant than small people. They're juicy and attractive at any age. They're as big at ninety as they were at twenty or thirty. It's not as though they haven't had their own share of let-downs and disappointments. It's that they resist the pull of bitterness. They refuse to sink into apathy, resignation or resentment, however tempting. They know that's the route to smallness, tightness and meanness. Keeping their horizon broad and open is more important. Fundamentally it's this glorious independence of thought that makes them so interesting. They're non-conformists – genuine original thinkers. It is this that makes them stand out among small people.

Socrates, Christ, Galileo, Joan of Arc, Columbus, Abraham Lincoln, Thomas Jefferson, Gandhi, Martin Luther King, our history books are full of the stories of big men and women, with big ideas, who were shot down – literally or figuratively – by smaller people. Smaller people laughed at them, locked them up, or gunned them down. But the world needs big people; people who are generous, principled, committed, and open to thinking and acting in new ways to solve problems and seize opportunities. We have big problems, and we need big solutions. We need people who can see a better world beyond the status quo, beyond their own personal one.

A 'small person' is not a person who necessarily has a low position or title, or little money or education. A small person is often a good person, a hard worker, a perfectly good friend. What makes someone small is simply that they see life in very small terms. A small person doesn't see very far beyond his own life, his own organization, his own time and place. He avoids change, clinging to the way things are. A small person sees things in terms of his own power, comfort or convenience. For a small person, cosiness is paramount.

Small people are usually very meek and rigid in their outlook. They don't believe in themselves, or if they do believe in themselves, they *only* think of themselves. They don't think of themselves as caring, sharing beings, intimately connected to the bigger world. They don't know how to fulfil their own needs so they don't have the compassion left over to think of anyone else's needs. Reconciling your own needs, fears and insecurities lets you become bigger so you have energy left over for the benefit of others. For the most part, people are small and insecure. They have little time for others. They're too mean and small to really care about anything beyond their own protection and security. A small person's life may be no bigger than his immediate wants, needs and fears. How often have you overheard café conversations where friends talk endlessly about their lives, their property, their relationships, their feelings, their weight, their job? You can see they're self-obsessed. A large part of developing bigness is developing a magnanimous goodness within you that supports others with kindness and compassion. It is by being kind and supportive and loving that you become big – and bigger. There are a hundred times more small people than big people in the world. They're everywhere, at every level of society, in every kind of business and government and non-profit organization. In the 1930s they made up the army of the Third Reich.

Paradoxically, World War II also called forth bigness in huge numbers of people throughout the world. In 1940 Winston Churchill called on British civilians to come forth and join his new fighting elite, the commandos. They came from all walks of life – doctors, decorators, teachers, bankers, lawyers – to answer the call, with no military experience, willing to fling themselves into whatever was required. Bill Watson was training to be a doctor when he volunteered. 'I was about to train to save lives as a doctor, and here I was learning to kill people. But I thought we just have to stop this fellow Hitler.' At the age of eighty-one, Bill was awarded an MBE earlier this year.

More recently the events on 11 September showed us how heroic and brave anyone can be when called upon. The technology company executives who took action against the terrorists on United Airlines flight 93 before it crashed embodied an old American spirit — that of taking responsibility for themselves. Thomas Burnett, Jeremy Glick, Todd Beamer and perhaps others phoned their families to tell them they loved them and to say goodbye. Then they jumped the hijackers and the plane that was on course for the White House or Camp David. By being willing to sacrifice themselves, Jeremy Glick and his comrades saved thousands. They were not passive. They took responsibility.

Don't be daunted. I appreciate that those were exceptional times and situations. Everyday life doesn't generally require such extraordinary heroism. But the choice to stand out and make a difference in your own way is available to you day by day.

The smaller-scale challenges of everyday life still call on us to contribute. And the world is far from perfect. There is much that any one of us can do to make a difference. Being big, you'll always be aware of life beyond your immediate environs. So, whether you demonstrate 'bigness' on a public stage or in a more private way, it's all an expression of your spirit, of who you are. Simply choosing not to join the ranks of the self-obsessed is an affirmation of bigness in itself. Feeling connected to others and living in full knowledge of the world beyond your own sets you apart in itself.

But what is it that renders people small, timid and docile? Why the retreat, why the defences and passiveness? Why the willingness to fall in line for the sake of a quiet life? Smallness can be passed on, taught and encouraged by our parents and early authority figures. 'Keeping your head down', 'keeping out of the way', 'saying nothing', 'knowing your place' and unquestioningly respecting those in authority is part of the answer. But you can also shrink yourself by the decisions you make about yourself and life once you've had a few knocks and 'defeats'. Some people begin to feel that things are pointless, that they're helpless or worthless, that no matter what they try they'll lose anyway. Beliefs like these strip you of your personal power and destroy your ability to act. In psychology, there's a name for this destructive mindset: *learned helplessness*. When people experience enough failure at something – and you'd be surprised how few times this is for some people – they perceive their efforts as futile. They retreat and shrink their world to fit.

At the World Trade Center on 11 September the decisions people made in the sixty minutes between first impact and the collapse of the towers dictated whether they lived or died. Many people reported hearing a 'don't panic' message, which urged them to go back to their offices, while others were re-assured by security guards to return. Some did. They almost certainly died. Arturo Domingo of Morgan Stanley did go back to his desk but later escaped. He and some colleagues started to go down the stairs, he said, but when they reached the forty-fourth floor there was a man with a megaphone, telling people there was no problem and saying, 'Our building is secure. You can go back to your floor.' Shortly after this, the second plane ploughed into the building over his head. He was lucky to escape.

In a laboratory at Yale University in 1961, Professor Stanley Miligram carried out a dramatic and disturbing psychology experiment. He recruited people from all walks of life, sup-posedly for an investigation into 'memory and learning', but, unbeknownst to the volunteers, he carried out what has since entered contemporary folklore as the Miligram Obedience to Authority Experiment. Each volunteer was placed in the role of a 'teacher', then paired off with a 'pupil' (who was actually one of Miligram's collaborators). The teacher was instructed to administer a series of increasingly severe electric shocks to the pupil each time he made a mistake. Although separated by a wall, the volunteers could hear the pupil next door. And as the mistakes accumulated, so the protests from the room grew louder, turning from cries to agonized screams. Volunteers who started to demur were told that they had to continue; those who really kicked up a fuss were told they had no choice but to continue. Despite all the screams from the room next door, two-thirds of the volunteers were fully obedient, continually administering the maximum 450-volt shocks, even after the pupil's screams were replaced by an ominous silence. The results stunned everyone, including Professor Miligram. It seemed that ordinary people – professional engineers, care workers, housewives – could be persuaded to deliver lethal shocks to a perfect stranger by someone assuming authority. Following orders, showing unquestioning obedience to authority, abdicating personal power and authority – it is always a choice.

Bigness requires vigilance. Since you are an independent thinker, a free spirit, maintaining your personal power and authority cannot be taken for granted. Personal power comes from living each day with integrity and grace. It comes from knowing who you are and your place in the world. It means having standards and boundaries. It means saying no to people when necessary. Giving your power away happens when you become too concerned with other people's opinions, conferring on them an importance and a status beyond your own. Personal power stops you from ever feeling a victim.

There are positive signs everywhere that people are waking up and reasserting their power and authority. We no longer have blind trust in the medical establishment nor, indeed, the government. In the UK, both have been trying to persuade parents to accept that the combined MMR vaccine is safe, with absolutely no link to autism. We're not convinced. Mass vaccination now looks most unlikely. We have a healthy suspicion of genetically modified (GM) foods and try as Tony Blair and the Department of Health might to convince us they're safe, we're not buying. Consumer power is forcing supermarkets to take them off the shelves and restaurants to remove them from the menu. You don't have to dress in white overalls and take to the fields to make your feelings count. Multinational giants now have to get ethical if they want to have your business. Boycotting these giants' goods and services for a day can be your way of saying no to their environmental record. Everyday decisions all add up. They're the actions of a thinking person, one who knows they can make a difference. It's also you being big, reaching beyond your immediate personal world to embrace more. You've got room for it, you're making space. In extending yourself, you get bigger. You're never too wrapped up in yourself to notice what's going on around you.

THINK BIG

1. *Don't be suburban.*
   Suburban is a mindset, not a place. Suburbanites build hedges and fences around themselves. They pride themselves on 'keeping themselves to themselves'. Privacy and security are all. To be otherwise would be 'interfering'. When George Bush dismisses the Kyoto Agreement on global warming because it doesn't 'put America first', he's being suburban. You're bigger than that. You're a citizen of the world.

2. *Be a conscientious objector.*
What do you want to say no to? Protest and thrive. You get bigger every time you make a stand. Your personal power is affirmed. You can do it as you push a trolley round your local supermarket. Your choice of detergent makes a difference; paying twenty pence more for an organic pint of milk is your way of saying no to factory farming and yes to a better world. Act local, think global. Small people think only of the extra twenty pence. You know you're part of a revolution.

3. *Be magnanimous.*
Get good at listening. Put yourself entirely to one side and 'get' the other person's communication. Let them 'be heard'. Make a heart-to-heart connection. Connect with the person serving you coffee, or sitting in the next car. Break the ice. Smile. You can lift someone's spirits in an instant. The best conversationalists often say nothing at all. Put yourself aside every now and then, and never, ever have one of those café conversations. You're far too big for that.

4. *Have a vision.*
Live your life in a context, not a vacuum. What does it all add up to? Get some big ideas about yourself. Make your life more meaningful with a big idea, a dream. You're a person of substance. Whether you're running a global giant or setting up your own cleaning company, ask these questions: 'How can I serve?' 'What can I give?' 'How can I help?' Ask these questions continually and you'll make your life bigger than just making a living.

5. *Stay big.*
Life tests us. Refuse to let anyone or anything diminish your stature. Every now and then check that you haven't shrunk a little. Don't allow a let-down or a disappointment turn you sour. Let it go. Dust

it off. Let it wash over you without sticking and warping your character. Stay fresh. Stay open. Resist the pull of smallness. It's too easy an option, too common. You're far too refined.

Small is dull, small-town, suburban. Big is shiny, dynamic, charismatic, fabulous, life-affirming, global. You're in good company. You're part of the best club in the world.

Think big.

22

Grow Better

Warren Buffett is a legend. He's the man with the Midas touch who's just replaced Bill Gates as the wealthiest man on the planet. He's unbeatable when it comes to playing and winning on the stock market. And he's seventy-one. His long-term business partner, Charlie Munger, is equally razor-sharp and he's seventy-eight. They're both fabulously outspoken, hitting the headlines again recently when they branded corporate America and many on Wall Street as 'crooks'. At the same time, Mr Buffett said he could not recall ever having more fun than he was at the present time. The most popular radio broadcaster in the UK is Jimmy Young and he's nudging eighty. He was knighted earlier this year, fifty years since he first came to prominence. He has interviewed every Prime Minister since Harold Macmillan on his lunchtime *JY Prog*. One of my favourite novelists is Mary Wesley, one of the biggest-selling writers in the country, whose novels make brilliant BBC dramas like *The Camomile Lawn*. She wrote her first best-seller at seventy and is still turning them out now in her eighties. Dora Bryan has been receiving rave reviews for her role in the musical, *The Full Monty*, which has just transferred from Broadway to London's West End. At seventy-eight she's still strutting her stuff, doing the high kicks and splits that she's famous for. She's signed up for a year, despite a gruelling schedule of eight shows a week. 'It is not onerous, it's wonderful – it is a holiday to be in it,' she says. Mick Jagger, Paul McCartney, David Bowie, Raquel Welch, Robert Redford, Sophia Loren, Tina Turner, Jack Nicholson, Roger Moore, and Paul Newman are all 'senior citizens'. They're also eternally youthful.

Something's going on. It's not just that we're living longer than any other generation. We're living better. We're staying sharp and sexy as well. Joan Collins is still the epitome of glamour. Her new husband, Percy Gibson, is thirty-six. She's sixty-eight, going on forty-two. The thing about Miss Collins and any eternally youthful person (EYP) is that they all have such a strong life urge. Friends say Joan Collins has the youngest spirit of anyone they know, the mind of a teenager with the wisdom of someone rather older. EYPs know how to live well. They know how to enjoy themselves, make the most of themselves and get the best out of life. They genuinely have a big appetite for life, for living. They like being alive. They're just too young to die. They'll die young, whatever age they happen to be at the time.

EYPs are worth watching! Their energy, verve and life force is awesome. Helen Gurley Brown turned eighty earlier this year, but the driving force behind *Cosmopolitan* is still at the helm. In an interview she gave on her birthday, the journalist observed, 'She moves like a much younger woman – skipping across the room on tippy-toes with her clunky solid gold bracelets dangling. This, combined with her mental acuity, means that you stop thinking of her as eighty inside five minutes.' Gurley Brown is now editor-in-chief of the international editions; and since she took up the post, eighteen new *Cosmo* editions have been launched. She attends all the openings, from Croatia to Cambodia. And she assesses thirty-two of the forty-three international editions each month, judging from the layout whether they are following her format. This would be impressive at any age. That it's an eighty-year-old woman requires you to question most of what you've been taught about age and ageing. Helen Gurley Brown and increasing numbers of others are forcing us to challenge our assumptions about what it means to be thirty, forty, fifty, sixty, seventy and eighty. Fifty is the new forty and forty the new twenty-nine. Only a generation ago middle age was anything from thirty-five onwards. Now, that's 'middle youth' and it goes on until you're fifty, and beyond. There's nothing short of a revolution going on here.

Publishers, television executives and ad men are rushing to keep up. Earlier this year *Red* magazine held a seminar in London entitled, 'How to Talk to Middle Youth'. One of the speakers defined middle youth as a 'kind of attitude. It's women who have grown up without growing old.' In other words, you can be youthful at any age. It's a choice. It's a mindset thing. You can be fifty going on thirty-five. Look at the singer Lulu. In her Earl jeans, Matthew Williamson T-shirt and Marc Jacobs boots, she isn't dressing like a traditional woman in her fifties. She's a middle youther. Her image says: up to the minute, now, achingly hip, stylishly trendy, label-conscious. She's switched on – alert to what's hot, what's in and out.

Britain's highest-paid female TV presenter, Cilla Black, has just reinvented herself from a middle ager to a middle youther. The matronly doyenne of light entertainment is now to be found in skin-tight leather trousers and stilettos in Soho night-clubs – the very hippest, cutting-edge ones. One shocked, middle-aged newspaper gasped, 'In the smoke-filled haze and semi-darkness of this establishment, she could pass for someone much younger . . . her frenetic energy (she has been on the dance floor for nearly an hour tonight), matched by a svelte physique beneath that daring outfit, are not the attributes you would normally expect to find in someone fast approaching sixty.' Exactly! Go Cilla!

The old adage that youth is wasted on the young has become a nonsense, because youth can now be enjoyed at any age. Stephen Richardson, a Californian social psychologist, recently published a report titled *The Young West: How We Are All Growing Older More Slowly*, the central thesis of which is that these days, there's no hope of feeling grown-up until you reach your mid-thirties. According to Richardson, the age of thirty-five, once the threshold of middle age, is now merely the beginning of the end of a protracted adolescence. By the time people in the West have reached thirty-five, he suggests: 'Culturally and psychologically, they have become what previous generations recognized as fully formed adults.'

What's so appealing about being youthful and seen to be youthful? Young people are associated with openness to contemporary culture and to technology, a willingness to take risks, to stretch themselves, to be open to new ideas and beliefs. Old people, on the other hand, are thought of as set in their ways, rigid in their thinking, conformist and conservative in their outlook, more likely to be prejudiced and reactionary. Yet I know people of seventy who are fresher and younger in their thinking than some twenty-year-olds. An open, enquiring mind is yours for the taking, at any age.

Leading scientists and physicians have now come to the conclusion that the ravages of ageing are not inevitable and can be prevented or reversed. Trail-blazing studies from prestigious institutions are discovering that what we call 'normal ageing' is actually often due to deficiencies that can be readily corrected by taking antioxidant vitamins, minerals and herbs. Best-sellers like Dr David Week's *Superyoung*, Jean Carper's *Stop Ageing Now!* and Deepak Chopra's *Ageless Body, Timeless Mind* provide overwhelming evidence that most ageing is premature, due to poor lifestyle habits. Nutritionists and scientists have proved that cigarette smoking, late nights and dehydration from lots of alcohol and coffee increase lines and wrinkles. The greatest threat to your juicy, plump face comes not from the passage of time but the sun. Protect and glow. In his latest book, *Grow Younger, Live Longer,* Deepak Chopra outlines his strategy to enable you to reset your biostat (your biological age) up to fifteen years younger than your chronological age. Biological indicators of ageing include blood pressure, amount of body fat and muscle strength, hormone levels, immune function, bone density, skin thickness, cholesterol, blood sugar tolerance, aerobic capacity and metabolic rate. Your biological age can be very different from your chronological age. A fifty year old who takes good care of herself can have the biology of a thirty-five year old. Alternatively, a fifty year old with poor lifestyle habits can have the biology of someone many years older. The more you replace life-damaging choices with life-affirming ones, the better your entire state of well-being. It's not difficult to see that with a little effort you could look younger and feel livelier for a lot longer. Check out any of the titles I've mentioned on the subject. I particularly like Deepak Chopra's approach.

In the 1980s there was a vogue for the idea of physical immortality. Naturally, I was curious and attended the wonderful Sondra Ray's seminars. I got the book, *How to be Chic, Fabulous and Live Forever.* Whilst I'm not entirely convinced on the physical immortality notion, some of the other ideas made a huge impression on me. The most vital was understanding that ageing is culturally conditioned. You buy into it. You subscribe to it without noticing. It's just there. The cultural perceptions that surround you condition you to expect to look and feel a certain way at any given age. Test it for yourself. Close your eyes and imagine yourself ten years from now, twenty, thirty, forty. Unless you've already uprooted your societal conditioning, you'll find that, in your own mind, you'll probably see yourself deteriorating with each decade, in much the same way as you've been led to expect. You're on a path, the same one that the average person is on. If you don't like where it's leading, walk this way. If you're really serious about treasuring and maintaining your youthfulness, then you'll have to change your perspective. The conditioning of our society leads us to believe that as we grow older, we deteriorate physically and mentally. Breaking out of this conditioning is paramount. Grasping that it's not the truth is the first and most crucial step.

A brilliant demonstration of this was offered in 1979 by Harvard psychologist Ellen Langer, who effectively reversed the biological age of a group of men in their seventies and eighties. The subjects were asked to meet for a week's retreat at a country resort. They were not allowed to bring any newspapers, magazine, books, or family photos dated later than 1959. The resort had been set up to duplicate life as it was for them twenty years earlier. Instead of magazines from 1979, the reading tables held issues of *Life* and the *Saturday Evening Post* from 1959. The only music played was twenty years old and the men were asked to behave entirely as if the year were 1959. Every detail of their week was geared to make each man feel, look, talk and behave as he had in his mid-fifties.

The Harvard experiment wanted to challenge the way these men saw themselves. The premise of the experiment was that seeing oneself as old or young directly influences the ageing process itself. To shift their context back to 1959, the subjects wore ID photos taken twenty years before – the group learned to identify one another through these pictures rather than their present appearance.

The results of this play-acting were remarkable. Compared to a control group that went on the retreat but continued to live in the world of 1979, the make-believe group improved in memory and manual dexterity. They were more active and self-sufficient, behaving much more like fifty-five year olds than seventy-five year olds. Perhaps the most remarkable change had to do with aspects of ageing that were considered irreversible. Impartial judges studying before-and-after pictures of the men detected that their faces looked visibly younger by an average of three years. Posture had started to straighten, stiffened joints were more flexible, muscle strength improved, as did hearing and vision. Over half of the group showed increased intelligence.

Professor Langer's study was a landmark in proving that so-called irreversible signs of ageing could be reversed using psychological intervention. She attributed this success to the fact that they were asked to behave as though they were younger, and they were treated as if they had the intelligence and independence of younger people. They also had an exacting daily routine, with complex tasks to fulfil. The power of consciousness – the mind – to affect physical health is well known. Here, this power was directed to promote renewal and youthfulness. What's interesting is that middle-youthers do all of this instinctively. The likes of Cilla, Lulu, Joan Collins, Helen Gurley Brown or Warren Buffett act, think, behave and dress 'young'. They just don't 'do' old age or even middle age. They're 'now', happening people, alert to new trends, ideas, lifestyles. There's nothing remotely old about them.

GROW BETTER

1. *Act your age.*

   What age? You decide. Close your eyes and choose an age that spells vitality and aliveness to you. From this moment onwards think, feel and train yourself to see yourself as that age. Awareness, intention and attention will begin to move you in that direction. Dress youthfully. Dress for now, not what was hip ten years ago, otherwise you'll look dated. Look your chosen age. The world is changing, but not fast enough. You're stepping out of the way that most people still see a thirty-five, forty-five, fifty-five, sixty-five or seventy-five year old. You're beyond that. When people ask your age, say, 'What age do you think I am?' It's valuable feedback. When they answer, smile and say, 'Close.' If they hit your chosen age, you're flying.

2. *Stay fresh.*

   Remember there is much still to discover about the world you live in. Cultivate the 'beginner's mind' that is spoken of in Zen practice. Go to places or do things that are new for you. Stay open to possibilities and opportunities. Carry a positive expectancy in your demeanour. Stay open to change and potential.

3. *Strengthen your life urge.*

   Eternally youthful people (EYPs) love life. Make sure you do. Don't entertain the notion of 'retiring'. Design a compelling life and future for yourself, not one leading to decay and deterioration. Always have things to look forward to. Keep connected and engaged with life. Purposeful, meaningful activity is vital and life-affirming for all of us, at any age. Plan adventures that add to your life force. Whitewater rafting or driving along the Big Sur to San Francisco, with good company and great music, whatever does it for you, do it.

4. *Stay lean.*
Studies on rats found that a 30 per cent cut in calories stretches the lifespan by up to a third. Ensure your nutrition is of the highest calibre. Stay tall and supple with yoga. Keep body fat low with vigorous exercise. Chronic disorders, including cancer, are known to be postponed or prevented by regular physical exercise. Jenny Allen Wood took up running marathons in her seventies. Some sixteen marathons later, she's taking a break – aged ninety.

5. *There are no excuses.*
Don't ever hear yourself use 'old age' as an excuse for anything. Don't even joke. It's a popular, fit-all excuse. Don't buy into the inevitability or naturalness of deterioration and decay. Choose renewal and regeneration instead. Acupuncture, vitamins, herbs and homeopathy can all keep you in tip-top condition. Prevention is better than premature ageing. Don't neglect yourself. Understand that mind and body are a self-renewing battery. And the next time someone puts their poor memory down to 'old age', buy them a bottle of gingko biloba, which is good for memories at any age!

Think Miss Joan Collins – a childlike spirit, with the outlook of a teenager and the wisdom of someone rather older, not to mention a great body. Work at it. Be one of those eternally youthful people. Glow. Be a middle-youther. Don't even think about growing older.

Grow better!

23

Get Metaphysical

In 1952, Methodist minister Dr Norman Vincent Peale published a book, *The Power of Positive Thinking*, which became a worldwide best-seller. In it he detailed the power that mental attitudes and imagery have to affect one's life. Dr Peale's book was one of the many self-improvement books I was surrounded by as I was growing up in Northern Ireland. My dad was a phenomenally successful door-to-door salesman with the Hoover Company. He had little formal education, having left school at fourteen, but he adored the notion of self-improvement and getting the best out of himself. His teachers were writers like Dr Peale, Napoleon Hill, W. Clement Stone, Florence Scovel Shinn and Dale Carnegie. This was the mental atmosphere that I grew up in and absorbed. Much later on, in my twenties, after my father's death, I went back to these authors and discovered they were nearly all ministers with the Science of Mind Church. Reverend Louise Hay is its most famous contemporary minister and is probably familiar to you as the author of the 12 million copy best-seller *You Can Heal Your Life*.

I adore the philosophy of Science of Mind or Religious Science, as it's also known. The ideas go beyond positive thinking to include the philosophy that we are all responsible for the results we get in our lives; that our thoughts, feelings and attitudes influence what we attract into our lives. Beyond this, Religious Science sees God as Universal Mind, of which each one of us is a cell. God, or Universal Consciousness, is a vast ocean and we are all individual droplets within it. Many modern techniques and ideas of positive thinking, visualization and manifestation come from the mystery traditions of East and West. The teachings of Buddhism, Christianity and Islam are all powerful metaphysical teachings. From the Bible we know that as ye sow, so ye reap; as a man thinketh, so he is; and the karmic law of cause and effect is a fundamental tenet of Buddhism.

As a child I was familiar with the idea that we help shape our own reality through our thoughts and feelings. In my student days I abandoned all these ideas, returning to them with a fresh curiosity in my late twenties. I got to grips with the power of affirmations and visualization, manifesting or attracting into my life the people and outcomes that I desired. I learned meditation techniques and had great fun playing with the rule that thought is creative. I took courses in developing intuition, psychic development and spiritual healing. The better I got, the better – and quicker – my results. I found myself terrific homes at ridiculously cheap rents, endless clients for my practice in massage and self-esteem. And yes, I got good at manifesting parking spaces, and I still am! I was rigorous about my mental conditioning, choosing only the highest-quality thoughts for myself and my life. I spent a lot of time on my own and only associated with other metaphysically minded folk. I dabbled in Buddhism and learned how to chant for the fulfilment of my desires. Extreme, I know, but I was eager to test and live out this philosophy as clearly and power-fully as possible. I was selecting a different belief system from most other people at the time.

Fifteen years on, most people have cottoned on to the power of positive thinking. There's been an incredible shift in our approach to spirituality, sickness and health. The power of the mind to affect the body, for sickness and health, is scientifically accepted — it's called psychoneuroimmunology. You can even buy flower essences to promote positive thinking alongside paracetamol in your high street pharmacy. Positive thinking and subtle 'energy medicine' is big business. In the UK alone last year we spent £1.6 billion on complementary and alternative medicine products and visits to practitioners. Leading doctors like Bernie Siegel, Dean Ornish, Patch Adams and Andrew Weil have had a huge impact on our understanding of the extraordinary power of the mind in healing. Every day we are discovering more and more links between mental or emotional events and healing responses. Recent research has begun to show overwhelmingly that belief, be it in healers, miracles, shrines, drugs or whatever, is a major factor in recovery from serious illness. This, after all, is what produces the well-established placebo response, where a patient given sugar pills gets better anyway because he believes he's been taking powerful drugs. The reverse takes place when the 'nocebo' effect (opposite of the placebo) comes into play and the patient may become more ill as a result. This can happen if the people around you fear for your health and life, and you pick up those vibes. I heard of an aboriginal medicine man who, when asked what single thing he would suggest to improve Western treatment of life-threatening illness, replied that the medical system should 'stop pointing the bone'. To point the bone at people is to suggest to them that the spell of death is upon them.

Dr Andrew Weil has even witnessed the disappearance of a serious medical condition when a patient falls in love! Work by Dr Steven Greer at the Royal Marsden Hospital in London has shown that cancer sufferers who displayed a 'fighting spirit' were 60 per cent more likely to be alive thirteen years after diagnosis than those who felt 'helpless and hopeless'. Dr Rosy Daniel, former Medical Director of the renowned Bristol Cancer Clinic, says, 'Getting into the right frame of mind is of key importance . . . What does seem likely is that negative states of mind have a direct effect on the immune system and tissue functioning.'

So, we know that positive thinking is vital for good health and recovery from illness. The use of imagery and visualization to improve performance in sports, business and education is well known. But, what else can it do? And what do I mean by 'manifestation' and 'metaphysical'?

First, let's agree on the basics. Until recently our culture accepted a view of the cosmos that was Newtonian, mechanistic and materialist. Then Einstein rocked the world of physics with his theory of relativity, stating that energy, matter and the speed of light are all related. Over the past two decades, numerous books have been written on the parallels between modern physics and mysticism, specifically that the universe is made up of energy and fields, from which matter is derived.

We tend to think that a table or a book is solid whilst a sound or a thought is not. Yet each is merely energy or a vibrating wave form. It is the rate or frequency of vibration that determines whether we perceive an object to be solid or not. We can activate wave form at the touch of a button; we can flick a switch to produce light or heat, to turn on a radio, television or computer. We don't have to see these waves to know that they exist, and to make use of them.

Einstein showed that we are coherent fields of energy. We possess not just a physical body but an etheric, electromagnetic body as well. This force field is referred to as the human energy body, or the aura. Some gifted people can see auras and can distinguish different emotions as different colours, anger as a muddy red, love as a soft pink or green. Kirlian photography offers you a glimpse of your own energy field.

Your thoughts, beliefs and feelings all carry an energy. We instinctively know this when we speak of someone as 'heavy' or 'light', when we talk about a great atmosphere or a tense atmosphere in a room. We're defining the quality of the vibrations or 'vibes' of that person or those people. Dogs are spectacularly good at picking up on others' thoughts and feelings. They smell fear, and are likely to attack or withdraw when they pick it up. Even plants respond to people who love them far better than to those who couldn't care less.

Energy follows thought. You are manifesting, producing responses and results with your thoughts and feelings right now. You always have done. The particular frequency or vibration that you send out acts like a magnet, pulling to you more of the same. Who you are, what you resonate, returns back to you. Who you are is written all over you. To a sensitive person, you don't have to say a word. They'll read you like a book, the amount of fear, anger, insecurity, meanness, generosity, smallness or bigness. It's all woven into the very fabric of your being. You are your own calling card. Thoughts don't just have wings, they're boomerangs returning more of the same to you. And the more deeply rooted and passionately felt your thoughts, the more powerful and intense their energy and effect. It's like walking around with a sandwich board proclaiming and advertising for more of the same. Other people and circumstances will answer your call, pick up your vibration, tune into your frequency and align with you. Thought is pure energy.

Getting metaphysical means that you understand this universal law that thought is creative. Many spiritual masters have known this. Many know it now. The process of manifesting is an inner art that includes positive thinking, affirmations and creative visualizations. Manifestation is often explained by saying that our thoughts create our reality. The Book of Proverbs in the Bible says it succinctly: 'As he thinketh in his heart, so is he.'

Living with the possibility of generating what you would like to bring into your life is vital. Affirming quality thoughts and picturing the desired scenario are indispensable. Beyond these I have come to appreciate the need to *become* the very quality you are seeking, to embody its essence. To find love, first provide it. Generate it within. Give it away. Offer it to everyone you encounter. Be generous with the very quality you would wish for more of yourself. Become the very personification of love. If it's money, don't focus on the lack, the deficiency. See yourself as already abundant, in money and in all the other riches you already possess. Remember that you're going to bring into your life more of what you already are and are being. To have more prosperity, *feel* prosperous, intensely. Get on its frequency. Tune yourself in to it. Like attracts like. If you project fear and suspicion, you'll attract more of the same; generosity and trust, more of the same; kindness and compassion, more of the same. Concentrating on your lack of finances or any other lack brings you more of the same – lack.

When you want to change a deeply rooted thought, act in accordance with the new idea you'd like to have. Giving *paper* money away to an old lady begging for change leaves you with a feeling of incredible abundance, knowing that you can afford to be generous. You're changing your perception, your vibration, your *energy field* about money, about you and money. You're projecting prosperity because you're beginning to experience, to feel and see yourself as prosperous. It's now easier for more of the same to find you, to come your way. You're on the prosperity vibration. Poverty consciousness has its own wavelength. You're altering your frequency. Keep it there.

Observe people who are preoccupied with their safety and security. What they really feel is *lack* of safety. The more locks, chains, alarms and insurance they have, the more fear and suspicion they arouse, within themselves. They attract into their lives the very thing they fear most. I'm not saying be reckless. I'm suggesting that you avoid living your life expecting, looking out for, anticipating and preparing to be attacked, burgled, robbed and otherwise got at. Check the levels of fear you're walking around with. What you fear most is what will plague you. Fear will draw it to you like a magnet. Fear attracts like energy. That which you fear strongly, you will experience.

Some years ago I lived on my own in one of London's edgiest areas. I felt completely safe. I insisted on it, within myself, otherwise I wouldn't have lived there. I never entertained anxious or fearful thoughts, only their opposite. The same could not be said of my out-of-town visitors who found the area quite threatening. Within a day of arriving, sure enough, they'd have been bothered or robbed, their fears bearing fruit as if by magic. Metaphysics in action. Manifestation at work.

GET METAPHYSICAL

1. *Believe in God.*

Churchgoers live longer. It doesn't matter whether it's a synagogue, mosque, church or Buddhist monastery. Research tells us that if you're a believer, you'll live longer. Get spiritual. Get God on-side. See yourself as part of a benevolent universal God-force that is keen to support you. Work on your relationship. Don't go it alone. You are mind, body *and spirit.* Your life is sacred. Talk to God, ask for support. Pray. Just believe.

2. *Honour your fears.*
Respect the level of fearful thoughts you have right now. Leaving your car keys in the ignition is only for the advanced student! Don't make life difficult. Gradually work on reducing the level of fearful expectancy you're walking around with. Don't make a huge fuss if you don't materialize everything you want overnight. As long as you're continually upgrading, choosing the highest-quality thoughts and refining the quality of your energy, you'll notice the difference.

3. *Change the frequency.*
Every thought, every emotion resonates a particular frequency. To have more of anything, tune in to that wavelength. You have to get on the same radar as that which you wish to bring into your energy field. Reset the dial. Alter your frequency by upgrading your thoughts, feelings and actions. Personify the essence, the nature of that which you would like have more of. Love, generosity, abundance, friendship, whatever: generate it, wrap yourself in it, let it pour out from you. And then see what happens!

4. *Get peace of mind.*
Pay attention to your inner world. Step back from the outer world, so that your inner world can bring you the insight that you seek. For answers, guidance and wisdom look within, not without. Whether you see this as connecting with a higher power, your higher self, God or Jung's collective unconscious, go within. As a great writer once said, 'If you do not go within, you go without. Fifteen minutes a day of pure silence is your gift to you. No past, no future, no worries.'

5. *Allow for serendipity.*
Watch out for meaningful coincidences and everyday miracles. When you set your train of thoughts and energy in motion, watch out.

When you ask for guidance, listen. The answers could be in the words of the next song you hear, the information in the next article you read, the next film you watch, the chance utterance of the next person you meet. Allow for alchemy.

Bring a little magic into your life. You're nothing short of a wonderful miracle yourself. And if there's anything in your life that's not to your liking, change your *mind* about it, then demonstrate through *yourself* your new thought and you will move into that new reality. Your thoughts, your words and your deeds are your tools to manifest your desired reality. Try it. Come on . . .

Get metaphysical.

Epilogue
Have a Go

When all's said and done, I want you to get one thing out of this book. I want you to have greater faith in your wonderful self. More than anything I want you to get the habit of having a go. We're talking less fear, more chutzpah; less preciousness, much more personal power.

Go for it, in spite of what people will say. Take your risks and live with the consequences. Become a great 'getter-on-er' – a doer, a person of action. Follow through. Failure has no hold over you; you'll handle it. You'll always rise again, handling setbacks elegantly. No drama, no hysterics, you will just dig deeper into your unlimited resources. You've got incredible wherewithal, fabulous ingenuity. A crisis never leaves you where it finds you; you're taller and sharper afterwards.

You're stronger than the average person. When the going gets tough, you don't panic – you pause. You step back from the fray. You compose yourself. You figure out the best move, even if it takes a day or two. You think, what action do I need to take? You come back clear and level-headed. If you've lost your job, maybe it's not such a loss after all. Maybe you were bored. Maybe deep down you really wanted to move on, and this is the push you needed. Whatever the circumstances, you'll be composed and you'll bounce back straight away. Ideas and plans will start flowing through you. You'll make calls, get things moving. You will just get on with it. The fear and insecurity that haunts and immobilizes many people is but a blip to you. Running scared is not your way because you know that's a sure way to feed the fear even more. No, you front up to the challenge and it collapses under your glare. The greatest fear is fear itself — grasping that frees you from ever living a humdrum life.

You have a mindset that works for you, generating confidence, strength, optimism and peace of mind. You're building stronger psychological muscle every day, a thicker skin. You are smart enough to know how important you are, how important your life is. Everything you do brings a valuable service to your world. Whatever you do, make sure that you link it to the contribution you are making in the grand scheme. Whatever your business or means of earning a living, enshrine it within an inspirational context. Your life is far too important to confine it to the making and maintaining of money. You're above and beyond that. Link your personal success to the more powerful contribution that it enables you to make. If you're sweeping the streets, you are making the planet a more beautiful place to be for everyone on your patch. If you're driving a taxi, you're making a valuable contribution to your passenger's day, reducing their stress levels, getting them safely to their destination. They'll pass it on. If you're running the World Bank, well, you've got a lot of scope.

So, come on. You know what they say, life's for living. And the great thing is that you'll never end up with a limited life, where nothing ever happens. That's reserved for those who never do anything. The great thing about you is that you always

Have a go!

Inspirational Reading

These are books that I find inspirational. The list could have been much longer, but I think these are the most important ones. Enjoy.

Sarah Ban Breathnach, *Simple Abundance*, Bantam, 1997
Julia Cameron, *The Artist's Way*, Pan, 1995
Dale Carnegie, *How to Stop Worrying and Start Living*,
    Vermilion, 1997
Richard Carlson, *Stop Thinking & Start Living*, Thorsons,
    1997
Jean Carper, *Stop Ageing Now*, Thorsons, 1997
Carlos Castaneda, *Journey to Ixtlan*, Arkana, 1990
Deepak Chopra, *Grow Younger, Live Longer*, Rider, 2001
Deepak Chopra, *The Seven Spiritual Laws of Success*, Bantam,
    1996
Sonia Choquette, *Your Heart's Desire*, Piatkus, 1997
His Holiness the Dalai Lama, *Ancient Wisdom, Modern World*,
    Abacus, 2000
Wayne Dyer, *Wisdom of the Ages*, Thorsons, 1998
Gill Edwards, *Stepping into the Magic*, Piatkus, 1998
Shakti Gawain, *Creative Visualisation*, New World Library,
    1995
Louise Hay, *You Can Heal Your Life*, Eden Grove, 1996
Napoleon Hill, *Napoleon Hill's Keys to Success*, Piatkus, 1995

Napoleon Hill & W. Clement Stone, *Success Through a Positive Mental Attitude*, Thorsons, 1990

Dr Phillip McGraw, *Self Matters*, Simon & Schuster, 2001

Dan Millman, *The Way of the Peaceful Warrior*, H&J Kramer, 2000

Caroline Myss, *Anatomy of the Spirit*, Bantam, 1997

Caroline Myss & Dr Norman Shealy, *Creation of Health*, Bantam, 1993

Norman Vincent Peale, *The Power of Positive Thinking*, Vermilion, 1997

M. Scott Peck, *The Road Less Travelled*, Arrow, 1990

Sondra Ray, *Loving Relationships*, Celestial Arts, 1992

Anthony Robbins, *Awaken the Giant Within*, Simon & Schuster, 1991

Florence Scovel Shinn, *The Wisdom of Florence Scovel Shinn*, Simon & Schuster, 1988

Dr Bernie Siegel, *Peace, Love & Healing*, Rider, 1990

David Spangler, *Everyday Miracles*, Bantam, 1996

Neale Donald Walsch, *Conversations with God, Book One*, Hodder & Stoughton, 1995

Dr David Weeks, *Superyoung*, Hodder & Stoughton, 1998

Dr Andrew Weil, *Spontaneous Healing*, Little, Brown, 2001

Stuart Wilde, *Infinite Self*, Hay House, 1996

Marianne Williamson, *A Woman's Worth*, Rider, 1993

Get in Touch

I have launched my club, The Next Level, in response to the thousands of you who have found my first book, *Be Your Own Life Coach*, beneficial and wanted more ongoing motivation and coaching. The club provides brilliant value-for-money courses from myself and a range of superb coaches. Whether you want to Build Indestructible Self-Belief, Redesign Your Career, Reinvent Yourself or Enhance Your Dating Confidence, you'll find the perfect course for you. You'll also be able to join us live online every week in coaching sessions and discussions and network with like-minded people here and beyond. You can reach us at www.fionaharrold.com

I really look forward to hearing from you and until then I leave you with an old Irish blessing that I grew up with . . .

May the road rise to meet you and may the wind be always at your back.

Love and Best Wishes.

Fiona Harrold

Fiona Harrold

Fiona Harrold's earliest exposure to coaching was at the age of eleven when, growing up in Northern Ireland, her beloved father would inspire her with the likes of Norman Vincent Peale, Napoleon Hill and Dale Carnegie – the US founding fathers of twentieth-century self-help philosophy. Michael Harrold was a charismatic individual who breathed fire into her sense of herself, implanting the belief that she could do anything. This is precisely what she does for her clients – many high-profile figures from the worlds of politics, entertainment and the media. She also provides ongoing coaching and consulting to a number of businesses, and has recently set up the first volunteer coaching programme for teenagers in a London school with plans to extend the programme nation-wide.

Fiona's special passion is to make the world a better place to live by helping people discover and develop their own unique qualities and talents. Her intention is to take the principles of personal responsibility and individual self help to the widest public through her club, The Next Level, and its wide range of motivational services and courses.

Fiona makes frequent TV appearances and features regularly in the UK media. She is based in London.